The National Poetry Review
Issue Number Ten

Editor:
C. J. Sage

Assistant Editors:
Ashley Capps
Jill Alexander Essbaum

Reviews Editor:
Douglas Basford

Contributing Editors:
T. R. Hummer

Subscriptions:

Individuals: $20 per year
Institutions: $25 per year
(Please add $6 for subscriptions outside the United States)

Address **subscriptions** to:

Subscriptions
The National Poetry Review
Post Office Box 2080
Aptos, California 95001-2080

**TNPR reads magazine submissions in email only.
Please see website for the latest guidelines.**

For prize offerings and detailed submission guidelines, please visit
www.nationalpoetryreview.com

The National Poetry Review is a 501 (c) (3) non-profit organization.

The National Poetry Review is distributed in the United States and Canada by Ingram Periodicals, and indexed by *Humanities International Complete* and *The Index to American Periodical Verse.*

The National Poetry Review Copyright 2003, 2004, 2005, 2006, 2007, 2008, 2009. 2010, 2011
All rights reserved
ISBN 978-1-935716-07-5
ISSN 1543-3455

Cover Art:
Lebensnischen
Oil on canvas by Ulla Gmeiner
www.ullagmeiner.com

Contents

Poetry

Mary Biddinger: *Three poems*	5
Amy Graziano: *Ghosts*	11
Stacy Kidd: *Three poems*	12
Tom C. Hunley: *Self Portrait as a Child's Stick Figure Drawing . . .*	15
Sidney Wade: *Two poems*	17
Melissa Hotchkiss: *Mt. Mansfield*	24
MRB Chelko: *Two poems*	26
Cynthia Cruz: *Untitled*	28
Christina Hutchins: *Tinntinabulations above the Bay*	30
Jessica Piazza: *Kopophobia*	32
J. Morris: *Surface Tension*	34
William D. Waltz: *Three poems*	36
Marcus Myers: *Quiet Project*	41
Angela Vogel: *Three poems*	44

Reviews: 45

Dorine Jennette on Amy Holman

Amanda Auchter on Emily Carr

Melissa Studdard on C. K. Williams

Andrew McFadyen-Ketchum on Michelle Boisseau

Douglas Basford on Angela Sorby and Gerry LaFemina

About the Contributors: 61

Mary Biddinger

A Poverty

It wasn't a paper flower they left
at the crash site, but somebody's
underpants, dimpled with rain.

Pink, for forgiveness and speed.
Our apartment was the lost space
between a walnut's hemispheres.

Our bodies the sole inspiration
for Velcro, though we earned no
royalties, just clung all afternoon.

There was nowhere else to be.
The difficult times were upon us.
We spread them out like maps

then situated our bare selves
on top of them. Down the block,
colonials vomited their contents

onto the parkway. Box fans
must have been reproducing
in the bushes. Every house had

at least two, sometimes still
circling. One fan romanced
the leg of a dead hobbyhorse.

A shiver struck me, thinking
of our toaster oven evicted
from its den on the counter.

We broke into the abandoned
barber shop, but nobody cared.
You spun me in the chair. We

did not cut a thing. The red wig
stationed beside a mailbox never
grew on its own, or flew away.

A Trick Knee

My humor was not an ill humor.
The cables holding my bones to other
bones were most forgivable.

It's not possible to sink
into yourself like my car keys
into the swamp where I threw them.

The bones you rode in on.
The bones that rode you back home.
The secret is to keep moving

like you mean it. Peer over
your shoulder and a roof collapses
under the weight of its squirrels.

A collective bargain. You cut your
finger and I'll bleed mine.
The diagnosis: perfect health,

if not a hint of the remarkable.
Those cement blocks aren't heavy
after all. I'll save one for your

back. We'll move them downstream

to where there's no circulation.

Nothing left in the world to get down on.

In Which We Sense That We Are Not Alone

Various miracles of the most outlandish sort,
and nothing was too heavy to carry.
We had to crouch in the bushes with our nets,

so to speak. Unfurl our maple brown
hair with less caution. They lined me up again,
and the shabbiest bee ever created fell

into a cup of lemonade, almost finished, but not.
The lesson here was supposed to be in
pragmatics. My supporting materials long gone,

left behind the tree where you stripped
pieces of bark for our lunch spoons, then every
centimeter of cotton and microfiber,

faux lace made with care by a robot in Thailand.
Somehow, a hole in my butterfly net.
The scandal! Chaos in the conservatory, or else

just an extra ripple in an experimental
holding pond. Somewhere a bride tumbled off
the bejeweled saddle made for a pony

but stapled onto a sawhorse for safekeeping.

Our love was more like the ultraviolet
lamp my teacher let me demolish after class

when it suddenly ceased being a lamp.
There was absolutely no word for any of this.
When I say it was no longer a lamp

I mean that it became a something of a god.
The trees dropped their trash upon us.
We celebrated with our guns, or lack thereof.

Ghosts

When God takes a man he makes a baby,
    or maybe he takes three men and leaves

one woman torpified, if I made that word,
    I apologize, dear lord, for I am in your image,

it is only the porridge of the holy spirit.

When my husband takes money
    he leaves an aloe plant. I like the upkeep,

little water, the gel-feel, in winter some flower.
    Babies grow to resemble the men that God took,

their cheeks soft, their eyes and build, age-old.

What does God do with these men,
    and why do some of them linger

in pubs or near piers, like mistakes,
    half-sheen, destined to repeat themselves?

Studies in Late-ish Spring

Everyone has a different name for sugar

shack: shanty don't move me

no mind, no rain, too   much rain: blue

hydrangea.

Sleeping Train dreams with one eye

open: sway-like, water

like water, shower: an earful of facts

about corn. A feller

may watchman, may travelogue, may exhaust pipe.

May Sleeping Train jimmy

loose his stuck red truck &   huzzah!

the summer:

silhouette & yellow flower,

shimmy-shimmy: a bride   may blush.

air date

So there is an August
arrowing toward you & you
cannot sleep. Simpler
to rim where insides
are determinate. Green,
the muscle of resuscitation—
to green the hung
to dry, to love
the scene freed from backbone. So
the weekenders packing
years into sad haircuts,
into every black velvet
Elvis-once-sang-here-too & you,
decisive as a lawn chair,
checking math as if an apple
is to a fried peach pie is
to a late-nite
chicken shack on Denver Street, O

Ought Seven

All along the tracks & trailing all summer
long in pick & not

an eerie light. Weeds grown big because
they do & pick. May

not a half-dead half-brother
once tall in one town over.

Damn bastard & knew light chews its own
fences last year

& year before last. The dandelions
laughed & laughed.

Self-Portrait as a Child's Stick Figure Drawing on a Refrigerator

> "You are not what you think you are. You are something to be imagined."
>
> — Clayton Eshleman

Often I'm a musical instrument

that's afraid of the sounds inside.

My days consist of arrayed efforts

not to hear or hum.

I'm like a baby who screams

at first seeing his arms swinging,

unaware those whips flung

straight at his head are attached to his body.

Why are you doing this to me?

a man asks his body as it fights sleep

and the crucial appendage droops after a woman

says *Okay, why not*, after steak and lobster

and Hugh Grant's latest formulaic schlock.

So spent, his body mocks him; he can't

fathom how he ever lifted the long-stemmed rose

he gave her, now drooping a little, too.

In my son's latest drawing labeled "Daddy,"

my hairs are stray spaghetti strands,

my head an oversized triangle crushing my stick-thin frame,

and a briefcase weights my three-fingered hand.

Often I feel sketchy like that, as if all the wrong colors

spill over my faint lines and anyone could cross me out

just like that. I haven't always felt like a stick figure.

I haven't always been an instrument
left forgotten in its case. I remember a time
in junior high when Doug Dickerson passed me
a pornographic flip book, the male stick figure's stick penis
getting bigger and bigger and the female stick figure's
stick legs getting farther and farther apart
until the stick figure bed broke and something hidden
deep inside me broke through, broke my body wide open,
a strange inchoate music that wanted to come out.

Sidney Wade

Coat Screws With Grease to Solve Woe

It isn't tiddly,
this non-ironic

little bubble—
it's a heart

burn formation,
double

vision
in which

misprision
of verb

for noun
happily disturbs

the diplopia.
It's fiddly,

it's true,
on the slope,

slippery,

of lubricious

soil,
but it's also

deliciously
knurled,

bejeweled,
oiled

and slick
with hope.

Geep

The music
of the sleepy

day was
ravagingly

dull until
Michael reeled

up a geep
from the depths

of his considerable
intelligence

a geep!
a wonky blend

of goat and sheep
a medical medley

genetic fugue
they call chimera

another wholly
enthralling sound

we found
when googling geep

whose enharmonic
bleating in the end

rings oh so
sad   the photo

on the screen
reveals a downcast

baby creature
neither here

nor there
two bold

and mordant
sets of chromosomes

whistling fortissimo
through its patch-work

hide   a botched-up
map of silken hair

and wooly yellow
fur its forlorn

droopy ears
a study

in radical
embarrassment

I feel profoundly
sorry for this

border folly
this lonely little

instrument
of the ever-

expanding notion
of what's possible

but then I see
we're kin

the little geep and me
we're marginal

ephemera
intoning low

invisible messages
at the edges

of the known
to who knows

whom
the difference

between us
a matter of degree

the poet of course
a hybrid creature

of transport and remorse
an over-reacher

in semaphore
who knows that sound's

the gold in the ore
whose pleasure-ground

is linguistic welter
who rides like ice

on its own melting
to paradise

or to a stranger land
we don't yet understand

Melissa Hotchkiss

Mt. Mansfield
(from my mother's cabin)

Through woods a mountain peaks
Nope, tips the tops of trees

Mountain-scape as silhouette
Boundary, in a land

Where the wingspan technically varies
From one snowflake to another

In a land where blood suckers
Slouch in mud at the neighbor's pond

In a land where moose pies
Are not to be eaten

In this land, I feel sin
Oh, not the sort I can explain

Please, I mean the sort that envies
Patience of sap in long winter

Or the sort which wishes beavers
To return every year, instead of every two

True regret forms in extreme beauty

This cold fire pit to my right, for instance

MRB Chelko

A Parable of the Poppy

Even though she'd buried
all the planets and stars
in her garden, the girl
did not feel better.

So, she planted poppies
to brighten up her little house.
At dusk, when she finished planting,
a dog barked softly.

That night, she was crushed in her bed
by more poppies than you can
imagine—some with roots bigger
than the earth.

By the Peonies

For one short instant, a long time ago, my mother
became a swarm of tiny beetles—
1,000 gleaming black faces, she swayed
the green leaves. Now

she stands by the peony bed. The peonies
in bloom, white and pink, lap at her ankles.
If she reaches for even one, she'll let go
the children and herself and speckles of light
she thinks.

Cynthia Cruz

Untitled

Welcome to the dawn of the haunted.

Kingdom of what, or whether,
Or not, I wanted it.

The machine that measures beauty.
The machine

Is feeding into me.
An IV drip of ermine furs,

Marble baths, crystal chandeliers that hung
Once inside the Russian Imperial Palace.

Consumption, whether or not
I wanted it. Fashion and excess.

Decadence, and its magnificent diamond
Of glut,

Glittering its warm doom and contagion.
When I was eight,

The news stopped the morning
Cartoons for live footage

Of a man gunning down
My father. Armed guards and

Eleven years of ballet
Cannot stop me

From starving. Starving
Against the incessant rush

Of memory, the glut.
I swear

The earth is still humming.

Christina Hutchins

Tintinnabulations above the Bay

A bell is loose in the sky. In the hour of spoons
& forks soft clattering in someone's steel sink
of soapy water, summer's extending the day.

Loll, yes, I have. & wandered slick
terrain. I've bent naked to wash in a basin,
cool fingers of water linked a moment with mine,

& I don't care whose pulse this is, throbbing us
forth. Whatever comes this close must have been
gathered from radiant distances: monastery bell,

foghorn, the first star, very old rain.
But even a generous day turns away. The bridge-lights
come on. From here their garland is a dotted guide

of perforations, telling me where to tear the dark
away from itself. Can my hand make of one
the two? What, who would be broken?

One day you, too, might walk up
the thick suspension cable of the Bay Bridge,
half-pulling yourself by guide-wires alongside

the strung lights. Approaching the tower, the path

grows too steep to continue. Before you the cable
has risen nearly vertical. Like water in the moment

a swimmer hoists herself from the pool, wind wraps
your legs. Would you mind very much if I leave you there?
Fog has taken the top of the bridge away.

Jessica Piazza

Kopophobia
(Fear of fatigue)

The pension in Prague had no alarm—
we missed the early train we stayed awake
to catch. My fault, our doomed attempt to sleep
in shifts; I thought wouldn't doze mine off.
For us, no clear, Hungarian lake to see
the sun's eclipse; it shadowed us outside
the train, out-dulled by clouds. We caught our breath
in Budapest and fell in love— adored
this city, thriving on its brokenness.
A new museum, but burned-through tenements
were testament to how destruction does
not mean the thing destroyed was beautiful
before. Those dragging weeks we built and razed
each day, and nothing that we made endured.
Our statuary garden songs were frail
as monuments composed of candle wax.
Your sketchbook left on the Bazilka floor
like trash; my notebook sloughing ink in rain.
It was a mess, but we make art that's made
for drowning. On the bridge by the Danube,
that storm deluged the city as we ran,
outpacing it until it caught us, sang
staccato rain into our hair and fled
too frantically ahead. I never said

I loved that broken way you looked when things
went wrong. I should have. I'll never forget
the fire-chewed bricks, the statues saved from riots;
how they braved ruin, but we could not survive it.

J. Morris

Surface Tension

The sleek duck holds himself
primped and sculpted on the pond
while below, like galley slaves,
vigorous orange paddles
power the visible animal.

Imagine a brain floating
in the illusion of self-sameness,
unable to feel the work being
done beneath the waterline
of being, famously unable
to sense a cancerous rebellion
of slave-cells. Some insignificant
creatures, it's true, travel
light, on surface tension alone:
the water-strider, a mere bug,
cruises over the molecules
on six dimples, and never crashes
through, its destination
chosen for it by chance propulsion
and a breeze.

The natural order
may not hold the proper model.
Instead, take a thing made

in our own image: the television,

its penetrable screen sifting

only dust and the odd reflection.

I see through that. I discover

consciousness, violence, laughter,

apparent stories. The repairman,

though (should I ever need him),

ponders a thousand metal and plastic

parts, charged, hot, working,

or not.

William D. Waltz

Island in Dispute Disappears into the Sea

We're not so different
that your north is my south
or my anger is your passion fruit.
Until high tide we saluted
the same royal palm leaning
into a full breeze of birds.
We sacrificed our hammers
and our nails and our paddles
to the same hungry gods,
but that didn't slake their thirst
nor mine for I wanted you
to see the green flash of sunset
and that was only possible
if you truly believed
the sun did set and you know
the stars better than that.
It's a trick we play on ourselves
like when we paint
constellations on the ceilings.
We see what we know
is not there for fear of falling
from the high ground.
We have communed
with the reef and the volcano,
with the turtle, the clownfish, and the guava tree,

with the angry young parrots and
the blind who live in the caves
and came away saying
we knew the heart of the island,
the hearts and minds of the plants
and animals and slowly like waves
carving beaches out of cliffs,
what we stowed in our amulets,
what made us one, we cleaved in two.
Our dream sunk back into the sea.
We are now ten thousand small canoes
bobbing in the chop. With no compass
and no land in sight, we'll wait
for the stars to come out tonight.
Tomorrow comes our sorrow
in the sunlight of regret
when we'll finally have
what we wanted,
a country of our own.

One Maybe You'll Keep

Dear Reluctant Sportsman,
maybe you'll release one
into the watery teeth of the wilds,
a tiny capillary
of our great circulatory system.

Dear Familiar Face
in the Passenger Seat,
I saw you undressing
that comely cornfield. I agree.
Maybe we're more alike
than even our combustible
engines suggest, and if we are,
you hope the next truckstop
has a wedge of pie
to die for too.

Dear Cell Phone Radiation,
we arrive almost invisibly
on the threshold of distant
relatives like a secret cold front,
but our departure
demands much horn honking
and happy hands waving
all the way

to the end
of the on ramp.
Our relief,
an algorithm
of how lonely
company makes us.

Dear Rainbow Trout,
you're a pretty fish
and I wish we lived
near the shivering brook
and the sunken tree,
then maybe we wouldn't forget
how to leave.

Part Salt Breeze, the Rest Lighter Fluid

The clambake, half-baked, wobbly on the shore, sputtered
long before we doused the coals with seawater.
The moon left early, the stars never showed.
Contaminated quahogs teased us while the littlenecks broke surf
extinct like legless fugitives. It started with phosphorescent plankton
we couldn't name, and ended with shipwrecks we wouldn't blame,
burning half truths in the sand. Captain Cook made the same
       mistake,
I'm sure. Dear James, the lighthouse has drawn its curtain.
We're free to follow the red lights home or wander off on our own.

Marcus Myers

Quiet Project

I have a quiet project
that begins once the car
points homeward. I turn down

the stereo, letting
the winds talk to me
over the strata of factory

stacks, over the underpass
squatters who flash
their tired faces when-

ever the Canadas fly. Into the gray
winter sky they cut their jagged Vs,
so gorgeous is their work

to reach the warmth
limned on the day's horizon.
I scan the river bank

where the water crumbles
the dun-colored dirt, when the water
carries the city

reflected there no-

where, and that's why
I think of houses,

the old ones busied with a dust
on the empty mantles.
The eye has a quiet project

that has everything
to do with joy and nothing
to do with cables. I think Westward,

flatboat, or purple mountains
soundlessly and just as fast.
The quiet is the kind gained

and lost in routine. A falling
out of love and in again,
a looking too much or too little. I lose

the quiet until the bridge's cold blue
high blank curved steel
lifts the whole

heart-driven world—
or at least every last
one of us

who will listen—

up out of ear-

shot of the frozen river.

Sanitarium

> *They all end in fire.*

Twenty pivots after the bore d'oeuvres and flatter-me-
chatter, I'm cast as daft. Boo that! I've the brain
of a dipsomaniac, the stain of disdain. If the pilot is out,
I can't take the blame. Grim and grimmer, a primer
for the plank. I drank the stew, I bought the farm,
I plucked the rubaiyat by its arm. Fire up the fruit flies
while we woman-up the yard. Our nutty bash has come
unhinged: we dish, we dash, we swoon, we yarn.
We lo' disease, we burn the barn.

History TV

The telly's back-peddling documentary in pacific
time, and plying me to *Armchair west!* with its
Michigan heroine, its shandrydan. All hail the lime
worm sailed around on thistle! All hail the crackerjack and
his paper riddle! The neckerchief alone is worth a kernel
of surprise, though it's all been done before, fountains
dripping news the Romans sent on loan, Manifest Destiny
around the world to the left. Even greed's foretold:
The man who can't hold water constructs an aqueduct
and the band hums bars of gold. The galaxy's his
luxury; history's his graffiti. His gaffe is thinking
Desert could be outfitted completely. Nothing
left to pan for, can-can, or speak easy. Nothing
but to channel how his town lived briefly.

R. Van Winkle—

Check out your gnomes. They are the paprika
of landscape, garden variety boys
in distressed salut. They don't give a rip
about your old lady's manor. They are squatters,
mooching. Twenty years of deep sleep.
They peel at the post like rain dipped in rust.
If you must choose decay, note the difference
at least in *overlook* and *look over*.
All the sons in your image are taking
a stand, dirt nap admiring, ornamentally wived.
There were extra yards they might have gone,
but at working stiff stature, their lamps petered out.
May they awake in laborious times.
May they keep an idle foot in the fire.
You have all overslept. You're welcome.

Book Reviews

Amy Holman, *Wrens Fly Through This Opened Window.* **Somondoco Press, 2010. 58 pp. $12.**
Reviewed by Dorine Jennette

"Think of the woman who found her twin living inside her ...." So begins Amy Holman's poem "Her DNA Rhymes, Internal," regarding a "human chimera," or person with two sets of DNA. In *Wrens Fly Through This Opened Window*, Holman's varied subjects include contemporary news headlines, ancient etymologies, school bullying, architectural digs, unrequited loves, beloved dogs, and awkward slang locutions. Uniting the collection is Holman's laser gaze, an angle of perspective combining incisive wit and passionate observation. In terms of sound, Holman writes a spiky line, a pointed expression rich in musical bon mots. A sophisticated wit, she leans hard on line breaks, allusions, rhymes, and half-rhymes, so that even though the work reads quickly, eye and line companionably skipping along, one senses that Holman has wrung the juice from each word with both hands.

Holman writes skillfully about alarming events such as infanticide ("A Soft Explosion") and murder ("Killed"), yet it is often her poems that begin in etymology and idiom that offer the freshest surprises. These poems ground their lexical dancing in moments of social intrigue. "And Plus," for example, notes the redundancy of the title expression, then passes through algebra en route to gender roles. The speaker is startled by an androgynous couple at an art gallery, laughing in "sudden, infectious / bursts," "lightly made up with shaved heads and wearing gold lame caftans." The speaker is sure one is male and the other is female, but which? The poem concludes, "Best together, even if one might / do for the portrait." "And Plus" begins with an adolescent tool of parataxis in storytelling, but eventually, by a path that only Amy Holman could create, arrives at a moment of gender confusion delivered with Whitmanesque urban affection.

Another of Holman's excellent idiom-journey poems is "To Where," in which the title phrase—as in, "It's one of those / situations to where you have this need / to be accepted"—becomes "a scenic pit-stop":

> The preposition proposes we
> pull into someplace further away than the subject driving
>
> through to the predicate. Where to, I have to ask, and
> what for. I see a turquoise sale in the painted desert, and hear
> a parking lot argument ...

And off we go, traveling through landscapes wild and domestic to encounter "humpbacks / breaking through waves, or the slide of a copperhead from / a crawl-space." Holman complains that the phrase "to where" makes too great a leap, sends the listener on a wild goose chase: "I got out when you pulled your sentence over, eager to see / the vast red desert and buy blue-green rocks from / a flat-bed. I got nowhere." Yet the reader, in Holman's passenger seat, goes everywhere, and is happy to be along for the ride, even when the road gets rough, as when the poem concludes in Petroglyph, New Mexico, population zero, when "If this poem is a vehicle, my hazards are blinking."

Some of Holman's headline-inspired poems also travel a wandering road, most affectingly "Busted Pipe," which begins,

> The 11-year old boy who drove 200 miles in his parents' car instead
> of going to school reminds me of the Roman pipe found at the
> archeological site in England. He was unable to handle the bullying

at his school, so he left at 5:00 before his parents would rise for showers and breakfast.

Holman muses on the hidden sorrows and humiliations of childhood and adolescence, which adults cannot or will not see, "although I gather they try to know more / these days." She considers how adolescent distress, buried like the Roman pipe, conditions adulthood from below the surface, as in the construction crew who assisted the boy's escape by filling his tank when he ran out of gas. The speaker recounts her own torment at the hands of classmates, who

> ganged up on me
>
> because they could, and they were bored and picked on, themselves, at home, and we were learning about sex and it was ludicrous and had to be taken out on someone.

Into this line of thought, Holman weaves the tale of "working alder / pipes from around 100 A.D. still trying to feed the old hospital with / spring water," so that the hidden flows in the pipes image hidden inner and interpersonal energies. This deft poem has depth, like its subjects. It invites and rewards as many readings as one cares to enjoy.

Less rewarding are some of Holman's other headline-inspired pieces, like "10,000 Bees Crowd Wing of Plane at Mass. Airport" and "Dalai Lama Latte Hits Taiwan." These shorter poems swarm with overlapping sound work, rich in rhyme and other musical effects, yet there's little to them beyond their glittery surfaces. Even favoring Tibetan independence, it may be hard to get excited about the six-line "Dalai Lama Latte" poem that ends, "Do you kiss / his holy caricature and swallow, or wait, / like China, for him to disappear?" It's a good punch line, but the poem doesn't do much more than joke. These poems are so tight they feel cramped, as though the poet has over-cranked their screws. Holman's abundant wit is shown to better advantage in poems where her wit is a counterbalance to other forces.

Holman's control of the line is masterful, and her voice in this collection sings in a music mixing measures of Emily Dickinson's bounce and density; Heather McHugh's irrepressible hijinks with rhyme and pun; Marianne Moore's delight in collecting, through rigorous attention, objects and animals and moments of interest; and Theodore Roethke's whimsical, vulnerable sway. Holman's intellect is a joy to travel with, for she employs it with a capacious curiosity and skill in a variety of modes. Her pieces inspired by John Singer Sargent's paintings, such as "plein air" and "Perhaps in the Forest of Fontainebleau," offer musical invitations to dreamy dusk- and picnic-scapes peopled by tennis-playing artists and girls in white ruffles who "light Chinese lanterns / with long matches," where "we talk about how stories / flower in the rocks of difficult walkways," and "Soon, we'll take / the sheet that clothes the table in the olive shade."

Such dreamscapes require room to maneuver. As Holman says in "Cerebral Countries,"

> Sometimes the digital clock
> across my room is not a bright smear,
> but a mug shot of a golden retriever,
> or the etched refraction of some other
>
> kindness. Why let lasik surgery obliterate
> the mysterious etch-a-sketch of thought
> and optic nerve on sleepless nights?
> I like how believe has the same root as leave
>
> how disconnecting from the known

is the way to know.

The poet is most impressive, and most delightful to read, in the poems where she travels over wide associative distances, allowing space between her virtuosic lines for mystery to seep in.

Emily Carr, *Directions for Flying: 36 Fits: a young wife's almanac.* **Furniture Press, 2010. 80pp. $12.**
Reviewed by Amanda Auchter

"de-articulate, mirror / the lunatic bride, stork- / legged, painting her home in / lunatic // colours," writes Emily Carr in the poem "hinge (v.)" in *Directions for Flying*, winner of the premiere Furniture Press Poetry Prize. *Directions for Flying* functions as a pleasurably disjointed "how-to" guide for young wives. Included in the collection is a piece of paper, a "postscript" (as so titled) that informs the readers that

> The first thing you should know is that between finishing this mauscript (which she privately refers to as "sprawl") and writing these notes, Emily Carr turned 29, 30, 31…So I can only speculate on the person who wrote these poems. She was 28 when she started writing them, 29 when she finished. She moved from the Midwest (her childhood home) to North Carolina, fallen in love, had an abortion, eloped, made a suicide gesture involving Zoloft & sherry, and moved to Canada. She became, for the first time, a seasonal creature. She had forgotten winter, and, in the fog of her despair, moved straight into the thick of it, to a sunny, austere, cold province on the right hand of the Canadian Rockies.

The function of this postscript is unclear: a clever bio note, perhaps, or possibly a note with the intention of informing the reader about the context in which the poems in the collection were written. Whatever the case, the postscript, while at times humorous, others sad, falls flat and at times seems a bit much like a quick-witted gimmick. The postscript goes so far as to quote Canadian poet Daphne Marlatt as stating that Carr writes "the husband" and not "my husband," which is important because, "the husband is clearly her husband."

The failure of this postscript, which seems to be an integral part of the collection as a whole, is that it informs the collection in a way that leaves no room for mystery. The reader does not have the chance to discover the joys and sorrows of a new marriage, an abortion, depression along with the speaker and is instead force-fed the thematics that pull the collection together. This is disappointing in a way, because there is much to admire in *Directions for Flying*. However, the postscript nullifies what there is to uncover, the great journey of a new marriage that Carr asks the reader to undertake.

The poems in the collection follow the first three years in the life of the female speaker, newly married. *Directions for Flying* is broken into twelve sections, each named for a month of the year, beginning with April and ending with March, reminiscent of Plath's Ariel construction which begins with the notion of love and ends with the image of bees flying towards hope, "tasting the spring." Similarly, in Carr's work, the narrative arc begins with the undercurrent of pastoral lushness (April, the time of marriage) and carries the reader through the early, often difficult years of the speaker's marriage to end with beauty and renewal (March).

Directions for Flying owes much to the literary canon and almost every poem in the collection is after or inspired by a poem from another writer: Frank Bidart,

Nick Flynn, Mary Ruefle, Matthea Harvey, Lyn Hejinian, C.D. Wright, Anne Carson, and Virginia Woolf (to name a fraction) all make appearances throughout the collection. Directions for Flying is a smart work in the way that the "inspired" poems give subtle clues as to the mind of the poet/speaker during these early years of marriage. For example, in "child (n.)," a poem after Nick Flynn's "Cartoon Physics, Part I," Carr writes, "if a man runs off a cliff / he won't fall // until he realizes / his mistake," which is almost verbatim of the lines in the Flynn poem. However, Carr continues with

>this small heart.
>
>rocking
>on a toy horse, already
>stupefied
>
>toward oblivion.
>
>a grace note an appoggiatura
>a suspension
>gleeful

Here, Carr moves away from the inspired (or borrowed) line and presents the true dramatic situation of the poem: the world of the child, never born. Carr's work is at its finest when it pushes toward the authentic, when there is no influence from another work. An example of this is the poem "yolk (v.)," which describes the speaker's abortion. Carr writes:

he's gonna havta reach inside you.

he's gonna do it. you asked him to. he's gonna tell you how old it is. he's gonna decide when old is too.

then you're gonna wait.

you're gonna stand against the wall, in your paper gown.

you're gonna wait in line. wait for him to vacuum inside you.

you're gonna listen. the other girls, like a sorority, they dont consider this anymore than the Piggly Wiggly line. for all they know, they could be buying lipstick.

Carr's use of image and specificity here is sublime. The poem's focus is realistic, sharp, and tragic. Carr's darkly comedic lines ("they dont consider this / anymore that the Piggly Wiggly line") juxtapose smoothly with the horrific subtlety of the process of abortion ("wait for him to vacuum inside you.")
  "Yolk" is the narrative centerpiece of Directions for Flying. The speaker in these poems often likens herself, or versions of herself within the confines of the first three years of bridalship, to birds: sparrows, storks, anything winged. Like a bird, the speaker is in constant motion, both physical and psychological, darts both to and away from fear (of traditional feminine roles, of the abortion, of death, of loss). In "bathtub (n.)," Carr writes, "I create myself or else I panic." The poems in Directions for Flying are not merely an almanac of a young wife's first years of marriage, but a tender portrait of a contemporary feminine voice undergoing considerable choices, changes, and consequences. Each section of Directions for Flying presents three years: three Aprils, three Mays, three Junes, and so forth in which the speaker's world evolves beyond the image of "a young housewife

/ in a negligee tucking in / stray ends of hair" ("tiara (n.)") and into one of growth, of lessons learned, where survival of both the marriage and the life of the speaker exist within these tight, fragmented lines. "Our precariousness. love clings . // like a hookworm inside us. / eats. you have to know this in order / to live," Carr writes in "cocoon (n.)." These poems cling in their music, their detailed tragedies, the idea that even in love, "what humans build from what / is human" ("cocoon").

C. K. Williams, *On Whitman.* **Princeton University Press, 2010. 187 pages. $19.95. Reviewed by Melissa Studdard**

      C.K. Williams states in the preface to *On Whitman* that when he began writing the book a friend asked him, "What in heavens name is left to say?" This question, however, misses the point. The pleasure of reading such a book is not in learning something new about Whitman, but, rather, in seeing one brilliant poet through the eyes of another, a pleasure akin to finding Keats' marked up copy of Shakespeare's plays. On Whitman, in fact, purports to be a very different kind of book on the writer, and in most ways it is. Williams says, "I felt the need to clear the air – to approach the poetry as I had when I first came across it, to try to reestablish and reconfirm the raw power of the poetry in the context it was making for itself on the page, not in the range of all that lay behind it." He says, furthermore, that he didn't even want to revisit what Whitman himself had proclaimed about his own intentions. Yet, paradoxically, the book looks well beyond Whitman "the poet" to focus on Whitman "the human being who wrote the poems." Though this may sound like a minor difference, the distinction is central to Williams' approach.
      Williams acts as a detective, out to explore a mystery he can never solve: the source of Whitman's genius. His foremost concern – when and how Whitman first heard his music – kicks off the investigation with a probing and insightful vignette titled simply, "The Music." In language itself poetic, Williams intones, "we'll never really know when he first fully intuited, and heard, and knew, that surge of language sound, verse sound, that pulse, that swell, that sweep, which was to become his medium, his chariot – just to try to imagine him consciously devising it is almost as astounding as it must have been for him to discover it." Proving insolvability the most minor of setbacks, Williams plunges forward undeterred, fleshing out and honoring the mystery of Whitman's music. He talks of scraps of loose paper jammed into pockets, poems written piecemeal, an astonished Whitman stumbling onto something divine, something that only he can hear. Here Williams, whose scope extends far beyond Whitman to the nature of poetry itself, argues for music as the Prime Mover in poetry. Without it, all else is noise, just words on a page. Music gives the very shape to a poem, and within music the words are already simmering, bubbling, longing to surface.
      Williams looks briefly at some of the more technical aspects of Whitman's craft, as well – the phrase and clause as organizing principles, the chromatic Shakespearean rhythms and rhetoric, the King James parallelisms, the balancing of universal and particular – but in the end, he comes back to appreciation, determining that Whitman did something that "evidence is in no way able to predict" no matter how thoroughly one researches predecessors.
      Next Williams invites us to imagine Whitman in a state of bliss, having already discovered his gift. He likens Whitman to a jazz musician, sketching the image of a euphoric poet in the throes of brilliant composition and wondering how long he could ride this new lyricism he'd discovered. The rhythm was, like with a great jazz solo, so cohesive, unique and intense that it could contain within it shifts and leaps of theme, image and sound. It was a framework for Whitman's entire vision, which Williams demonstrates through biographical anecdotes and imaginings to be the vision of a prophet and true humanitarian. Williams goes on to show Whitman's importance to specific groups of people – especially women and homosexuals. Quoting from Ginsberg's "A

Supermarket in California," and an essay by Mark Doty, he calls Whitman a "courage-teacher" and someone who gave voice to "a class of men who had felt themselves isolated and voiceless." Yet if there is a flaw in Williams' book, it is in this specific biographical aspect—a lingering, tedious preoccupation with Whitman's sexual orientation, which is several times dismissed and revisited as Williams tries to determine whether or not Whitman was indeed homosexual and if alleged dates with women were legitimate dates or not, a preoccupation which at certain points becomes overly investigative and loses sight of its bearing on the poetry and personality themselves.

Although Williams (rightly) reveres Whitman's gifts as a poet and human being, presenting him as the very cosmos he was and is, he does not do so blindly. There is discussion of sham inspiration in later life and the mediocre journalism that preceded the exceptional poetry. However, Williams, who points out that most biographers at some point in their writing display contempt for their subjects, continues to revere Whitman, inclusive of his flaws. He points out, as well that other Whitman biographers continue to love, admire and revere Whitman well after they've learned everything they can possibly learn about him.

Much of what Williams discusses is the stuff we already know – the empathy, the creation of the "I," the inclusive phrases and clauses, the fact that Whitman's influence on others is much more important than anyone's influence on him – but Williams' manner of presentation is completely unique and more deeply insightful, human, compassionate and lyrical than most other such discussions. As well, he provides an interesting argument that Baudelaire, more than Dickinson, is Whitman's true literary counterpart and a more logical pairing for study.

In the end, this beautiful and creative look into the world of Whitman serves also as a look at the art of poetry in general, as Williams' extensive knowledge and deep mastery of the form shine through, page after page, vignette after vignette, to offer a comprehensive understanding not just of Whitman, but of poetry itself.

Michelle Boisseau. *A Sunday in God-Years.* **University of Arkansas Press, 2009. 100 pp. $16.**
Reviewed by Andrew McFadyen-Ketchum

Michelle Boisseau's fourth collection of poems, *A Sunday in God-Years*, recounts White America's brutal history of slave-ownership paired with its desire for reconciliation via the exploration Boisseau's ancestry, dating back to 17th Century Virginia.

Obsessed with the transitory nature of this conflict between White and Black America, *A Sunday in God-Years* opens with the prefatory "Birthday" wherein Spring is "full of exuberant ruin" and life is defined as "a frantic flight across a crackling room / where the clan feasts, harps gleam and the storm / is carefully forgotten." Rebirth, war, fire, flight, and institutionalized denial: these are the obstacles "Birthday" declares must be overcome in the poems that follow. Luckily, Boisseau has no illusions regarding this task, asking near the end of the first section "…me, grandchild who makes herself the hero / since she's the teller of this tale… / How can I begin to recount / [our] sins, a million ships on every ocean?"

Boisseau establishes herself as a master of transition and symbol in the title poem which opens with a depiction of God turning over in his afternoon nap to see the earth in an accelerated state of geological evolution, "continents crashing / and mountains popping up." She then zooms in with a mid-sentence stanza break, focusing on a small "chunk / of limestone I plucked / from a wall fading into the woods / …shaped / like Kentucky" and zooms out to a bend in the river where "a runaway could hide / studying the floes". The poem ends with a return to the snoozing God morphed into the more Pagan "younger sun" disinterested in "these grainy eons, plunder / imbedded with the trails and shells / of creatures seen by no eye."

This mastery of transition and symbol comes in handy in the next poem, "A Reckoning." 21 pages of individually titled sections, it opens with "The Debt," which compares Boisseau to a portico which depends on the stones that give it structure, asking "What do you owe when you find your / name on a parchment deed?" "Reward" directly lifts the Reward Notice her great grandfather placed in the Richmond Enquirer when one of his slaves escaped in 1834, and "Two Wills in Old Virginia" quotes word-for-word the family wills that passed slaves and their children to future generations. These documents overlap with depictions of early America when the future planes states "became Indian territory and ragged / bands of Shawnee were run out of Ohio" in "Meanwhile." "Brown Study" compares the Kansas River's flow south to those fleeing Lawrence, Kansas during the Pottawatomie Massacre in 1856, and "The Subscriber" depicts a bounty hunter beating free blacks he hopes are escaped slaves.

Throughout "A Reckoning" an image recurs of Boisseau attempting to capture the essence of this American tragedy and the burden that still weighs so heavily upon us 150 years after emancipation. Seeking out the ruins of slave barracks at what was once the Boisseau plantation, she finds "not The House Where They Lived! // No be-lilaced cellar hole… / Nothing to weep over… // Instead, big as an airplane hangar, / a garage for backhoes and spreaders… / where the big house might have stood." At the heart of this burden is the desire for a return to the past but in the actual, physical world. Of course, as time and "progress" slowly but surely destroy the physical evidence of America's misdeeds, this return becomes more and more elusive. The closest Boisseau can get to this return is via the superimposed vision of her own poetry— an ingenious move poetically but one that comes with a woeful realization: we cannot return, we cannot forget, we cannot be fully forgiven.

This woeful epiphany is on display in the final sections of "A Reckoning." "Apologies," equates these sins to the "millions" of slave ships that crossed the Atlantic for the New World; the resulting guilt as bound to White America as silt and oceans to the earth in "Field Guide to American Guilt." In the penultimate section, her great Grandfather's escaped slave admonishes Boisseau's attempts to understand or even lament his struggle: "Thought you try to puppet me / what happened to me is not / for you to know." In the final section the Boisseau plantation burns to the ground.

The only problem with this first section is that the narrative is given too much power, the more lyrical elements of the line that make poetry unique from prose overpowered by storytelling. This is not to say that this first section isn't poetry or that it's not worth reading. This is simply to suggest that it's not as engaging on the level of the lines as, perhaps, it should be. Ironically, this problem is reversed in the second section, which (save for three of its 23 poems) abandons narrative for a more lyrical approach to Boisseau's lamentation of history's erasure in lines like "The iron taste of what / they did is laid down / in twisted bark, bit by bit" ("Outskirts of Lynchburg") and "The rowboat is slapped by the harried lake. / The oars bob and beckon out of reach / …Today the future isn't what it used to be" ("Sandcastle Guarded by a Cicada Shell"). Typically, shifting to the lyrical would be a good idea, but these poems go a little too far. They stand perfectly well on their own but depend too heavily on what is established in the first section without utilizing the story-telling tools Boisseau has already so richly deployed. As a result, the poems of the second section bleed together and much of the book's momentum is lost.

The third and final section is dominated by "Across the Borderlands, the Wind," a nine-page, elliptically sectionalized depiction of the brutal guerilla warfare between the Confederate bushwackers and Union jayhawkers over the indoctrination of slavery in Kansas, eventually igniting the Civil War. It's a difficult poem to follow, leaping in time, place, and speaker so often and quickly that, without the end notes, most readers will be completely lost. It also might be the best poem in the book, revealing how this seemingly resolved conflict within White America is anything but— "the football and basketball rivalry between the Universities of Missouri and Kansas…still often referred to as 'The Border War'"; the celebration held each year in Blue Springs, Missouri called as early as the 1990s the Bushwacker Festival.

But "Across the Borderlands, the Wind" suffers from the momentum gained by the first section and lost by the second. It requires an energetic reader, one willing to allow a poem, first, to depend on end notes and, second to actually apply these notes back to its elliptical approach. If Boisseau finds such readers, this book is quite an accomplishment, starting with the desire for reconciliation between White and Black America and ending with the realization that the conflict between White America itself has been the problem all along. If she doesn't, then this book is a failure: the balance between narrative and lyric never reached; the potential for this collection unrealized.

This leaves one wondering if this "failure" is, in fact, Boisseau's achievement, this failure eerily similar to that of The New World. Of course, we'd have to trust Boisseau quite a bit to read *A Sunday in God-Years* this way. Only time will tell.

Angela Sorby, *Bird Skin Coat.* **University of Wisconsin Press, 2009. 94pp. $14.95. Reviewed by Douglas Basford**

Angela Sorby's 2009 Brittingham Prize winner, *Bird Skin Coat*, is her second collection, the decade between it and *Distance Learning* having been bisected by the publication of a critical book. *Schoolroom Poets* (UNPE, 2005) is a revealing picture of the circulation of poetry in classrooms between the Civil War and World War I. Much of the world is infantilized in the bulk of the texts taught during that time, Sorby argues, and even the selections of Dickinson that eventually crept into curricula suffered from their context. Inexplicably sandwiched between passages idealizing William Cullen Bryant's birthplace and early home life, one such poem, "I'll tell you how the sun rose, −" is published under a title ("The Day") that saps much of its energy. The second half of the poem, detailing the rush of colors at sunset as a cluster of slightly unruly children eventually called in from play by a "Dominie in gray," Sorby finds to be "more theologically and epistemologically skeptical, but it is also, as if to balance its serious themes, cuter" than the first half.

Sorby is theologically and epistemologically skeptical herself, and like Dickinson any "cuteness" in her poems lingers as only the memory of itself in service of her intricate thought. In "Rose," for example, a little girl on a tricycle charmingly "plows past" a blooming rose, as "she's all about Disney: / Snow White, Sleeping Beauty." Half-watching her are three teen fathers, one of which is ostensibly hers, and as we consider his dissipation from drink we are not meant so much to lament the looming loss of innocence, which would be a truly trite move, as to marvel at the opusculum paedagogum of the ever-widening sphere of influences. His drunk singing is like the roar of sewage beneath the street, roaring out into the Great Lakes, overflowing, and we all keep it overflowing. The child will grow into that dubious virtue of silence, Sorby implies, and the rose, too, learns its lesson: "*Don't deepen, / don't redden, keep still // like a bead of water / in an enchanted // state without hills.*" What kind of happiness is available if we collectively tamp down our spirits?

The answer, at first, appears to be that we can't expect much. The explanation of the title of the collection comes in the form of a conservation note from the British Museum, which explains that "birdskin clothes are light, warm and waterproof, but they tear easily." Attempts at repair of one such parka by adhering Japanese tissue paper and goldbeater's skin could not allow it to be exhibited for fear of "further damage and loss of feathers." With such fragility, we will only catch traces, even if only indirectly, and try to hold it together in some semblance of a solid thing which we would be fools to put on display. And yet we do.

In the title poem, we find the speaker in a fender-bender on an icy off-ramp, exchanging names with the other driver. Anyone who has been in an accident knows the enervated sensation in the torso and limbs, and Sorby here gives it metaphysical force, landing on the hard question, "Do the drivers deserve / their down coats?" By what fatedness, by what right, by what dumb luck have they happened on what shields them? In perhaps the most moving and most figuratively, most intertextually challenging passage of the book,

> She notes with wonder
> how her parka fits her perfectly
> the way a dove's skin holds
> the whole bird together.
>   Fate
> is not a thing with feathers,
> it's old, bald, and blind,
> a pope who can't decipher
> the man's name,
>   *David Pratt*,
> as he scrawls it on scratch paper.
> But the woman reads: *David*,
> Yahweh's beloved. She has never felt safer.

A parallel drawn forth by the coats' congruities in form-meets-function, a connection by mere namesake, an almost unwitting leap of faith. That birdskin parka is all that shields us from oblivion in its many forms, happiness comes as some faint short-lived stability amid raging vicissitudes.

This preoccupation with what Frost called a "momentary stay against confusion" serves Sorby well in her collection, particularly in two poems that appeared in these pages some time ago. Again, in "Whose Woods These Are," she places the figure of fate prominently:

> The alderman leaflets:
> a REGISTERED SEX OFFENDER
> is living in a duplex on the corner,
> buttering toast (inoffensively?)
> while the old Shakespearean wheel of fortune
> falls off a passing Camry.

The skittering hubcap must come to a halt, something must happen. The sense of threat never reaches a fever pitch, as this circumstance has become such a commonplace, but Sorby forays into foreign territory, not merely imagining "our grave Offender" engaged in quotidian activities, but also trying to account for that which impels him—and us— towards the unspeakable: "but the storms are neuromuscular—// dark and deep // the storms are in our bodies as we sleep."

Threat from without, threat from within, can we ever suss out what will happen, prevent it from happening? In the second poem published in these pages, Sorby turns to chickens, with daffy bit of humor, splicing Chicken Little with David Guterson: "Sky Falling on Cedars" begins with the speaker discovering her father's advice for poultry farmers and careens to the climax, a comic "translation" of the terrified, magnified "cluck" of chickens as they are transfigured by an earthquake into Blakean angels, spouting prophecies.

If the sky's not, in fact, falling, then what are we so sensitive to, even hypersensitive to, exactly? Our lives can be read like tea leaves only by the perceptive few and only at incongruous moments. In the ironically titled "Prosperity," we confront Lacan, who seemed to have an answer for everything in the human psyche, but whose own impenetrability oddly enables the speaker to confront her friend's near-suicide. Whispering to him in the shed where he has locked himself with a gun, she finds the unsettling subtle satisfaction in finding the wrong words for the right situation, hissed through the thin metal: "You've never even had sex." He drops the gun. Sorby's poetry has that kind of effect, taut yet delicately compassionate, holding us together, keeping us warm, for as long as humanly and materially possible.

Gerry LaFemina, *Vanishing Horizon*. **Anhinga Press. 2011, 92pp**
Reviewed by Douglas Basford

   When a poet reaches his 12th book of poetry, as Gerry LaFemina has, the reviewer would do well to conduct a retrospective of all that work. In many ways, however, *Vanishing Horizon* does much of that work already, not just in revisiting themes and subjects familiar from previous collections—punk rock, Zen Buddhism, puppy love, family life, urban life, sex—but also in explicitly invoking the retrospective glance. It is not, however, some conventional inert nostalgia that LaFemina seeks or excels in, but instead hell-for-leather spiritual recalibration.
   Or at least that's what he has hoped for all along, having keenly felt the futility in playing a "secular monk." That admission comes in one of two poems in the collection labeled as "Perspective," the one set in New York City, the other in St. Thomas. By the time we reach these poems, we are already keenly aware of his reluctant falling out with all manner of claims to the spiritual life: omens are not omens, he no longer believes in miracles, though he can nevertheless, when a water stain resembling the Virgin Mary becomes a pilgrimage site, marvel at how "so many people hold vigil there"—the line breaks such momentum there that we can't be faulted for half-wanting, half-hearing it continue "so many people hold vigil / that…" That what? What is it that we want to happen with such showing forth of dire spiritual need? Observing them all, from those that "genuflect like birds" to a baseball team with their caps that almost impotently "now sag in their hands," LaFemina reads a different life for the young men than the elders "reverently, passionately waiting" in Auden:

> They look toward the puddles & are surprised by their reflections.
> They say little to each other, astonished by what they've gotten to see
> in this hollow beneath a highway
>   within that well-lit city.

The power of these lines lies in the careful management of ambiguity: were the players astonished by the water stain or by their reflections? Were the reflections a sudden interruption of banality, or did the puddles touch off what the "miracle" couldn't? The intricacies of perspective-gaining run throughout, though perhaps not as memorably than in "Perspective: New York," where after having assessed the money changing hands during pick-up games he and an unnamed other lean against the fence, watching and reminiscing. Called out for some two-on-two, LaFemina and companion seem to balk:

> What will we say? How good's our give-and-go?
> The moon small as a half-dollar so it's hard to believe
> men ever leapt on its surface & stared down
> at the earth, trying to make out the lights of New York.

That impossibly fast change in perspective is not facile precisely because it is filtered through disbelief and desire together, and because that desire is not his own, exactly. LaFemina does wonders when he lets others inhabit and express their desires and pleasures, such as when he gives a homeless man an apple: "Mmm delicious, he said, delicious like a chorus"
   LaFemina takes cues from the plainspokenness of Rexroth, Corso, and Stephen Dunn, siding with them when it comes to the intersection of disillusionment and

enthusiasm. In "Pineapple," a poem that sticks it to Stevens's impersonal denial of the erotic (see Mark Halliday on this point) and both playfully ribs and channels Williams, he joyously revisits his days as a punk rocker, delighting in the slippery analogy between punk girls and pineapples, the spiny tough exterior, "a studded leather jacket // zipped tight." The real charge of the poem comes in the brash but sure unfolding of exactly what we predicted, that the "golden light" inside of the "fruit" would be tender and delicious:

> wildy unexpected until eaten,
> doled out in pieces & in rings,
>
> the juice sticky on my chin
> so sweet & fresh, so acidic.

This "eating" metaphor is not just freewheeling or bacchanalian hedonism, though there is no shortage of that here, but almost more assuredly punk attitude (looking at us square in the eye as he does something that he knows he's not supposed to do in a poem) and, more to the point, a deliberate stripping away of deadening layers of socialized experience, almost like a series of phenomenological reductions. In this way, believe it or not, the poem—and indeed the multiple occasions when the word "delicious" appears in the book—ends up becoming a tribute of sorts to Stevens in the end, who wanted to entice us into a kind of Heideggerian primary experience of a thing. LaFemina topples us with that joy, then, of the "delicious," a word that too often feels dictated to us by pop culture as what must be said when something is delicious.

Even as he yearns for unencumbered experience, LaFemina is adept at showing how the things of this world point toward it, even the commercial. A "proof of desire" might be the "empty sail of a condom wrapper," the dissipation of steam above mint tea "the sublime or something like it." And perhaps most tellingly: "I want to walk into enlightenment / as if it were a shop to enter." It is no wonder, then, that LaFemina seems always to be on foot, even when rubbing against Buddhism's encouragement that enlightenment be achieved seated, in the "most table and peaceful of the four postures." He is a flâneur of our age and places, brightly stepping through streets and along shores, his spiritual dilemma ours as he buys coffee and a donut to "comfort himself":

> A block farther I pour that coffee
> into the gutter, watch its weak bitterness steam.
> I waste
>   so I shall want again. In this way
>
> I'm so American, & in this way, too, I'm disappointed
> by a cathedral's bolted doors, frost
> on its stained glass. Such avoidance.

_____The National Poetry Review

About the Contributors

Amanda Auchter is the founding editor of *Pebble Lake Review* and the author of *The Glass Crib*, winner of the 2010 Zone 3 Press First Book Award and of the chapbook, *Light Under Skin* (Finishing Line Press, 2006). A former Theodore Morrison Poetry Scholar for the Bread Loaf Writers' Conference, she has received awards and honors from *Bellevue Literary Review*, *BOMB Magazine*, *Crab Orchard Review*, and others. Her writing appears in *American Poetry Review*, *Court Green*, *Indiana Review*, *The Iowa Review*, and elsewhere. She holds an MFA from Bennington College and teaches creative writing and literature at Lone Star College-CyFair.

Douglas Basford's work has appeared in *Poetry*, *Subtropics*, *American Poetry Journal*, *Smartish Pace*, *H_NGM_N*, *Diagram*, *Two Lines*, *The Hopkins Review*, *The Texas Review*, and elsewhere. He teaches at SUNY-Buffalo, and co-edits the online journal *Unsplendid*.

Mary Biddinger is the author of *Prairie Fever* (Steel Toe Books, 2007) and the chapbook *Saint Monica* (forthcoming with Black Lawrence Press). Her poetry has recently appeared or is forthcoming in *32 Poems*, *Center: A Journal of the Literary Arts*, *The Collagist*, *Copper Nickel*, *diode*, *Gulf Coast*, *The Journal*, *North American Review*, *Passages North*, and many other journals. She is the editor of the Akron Series in Poetry, and co-editor, with John Gallaher, of the new Akron Series in Contemporary Poetics. She also edits the independent literary annual *Barn Owl Review*, and directs the NEOMFA: Northeast Ohio Master of Fine Arts in Creative Writing.

MRB Chelko is a recent graduate of The University of New Hampshire's MFA program and Editorial Assistant of the unbound journal, *Tuesday; An Art Project*. She has poems in current or forthcoming issues of *AGNI Online*, *Court Green*, *DIAGRAM*, *Forklift, Ohio* and others. Chelko's poems have been featured on *Verse Daily* and nominated for a Pushcart Prize. Her chapbook is *What to Tell the Sleeping Babies* (sunnyoutside, 2010). She lives in Central Harlem with her husband, Nick, and dog, Chuck.

Cynthia Cruz's first collection of poems, *Ruin*, was published by Alice James Books in 2006, Her second collection is forthcoming from Four Way Books. Her poems have appeared in *The New Yorker*, *The American Poetry Review*, *Boston Review*, *Kenyon Review*, *The Paris Review*, etc. She has taught writing and literature at Sarah Lawrence College, in the Rutgers MFA Program, the Juilliard School. Fordham University, and Eugene Lang College and is the Hodder Fellow in Poetry at Princeton University for the year 2010-2011.

Amy Graziano is a graduate of the MFA program at Southern Illinois University at Carbondale. Her work has appeared in *DIAGRAM*, *Flashquake*, and *Blue Earth Review*.

Tom C. Hunley is an associate professor of English at Western Kentucky University and the director of Steel Toe Books. Among his books are *Tom C. Hunley Greatest Hits* (Pudding House, 2010, Poets Invitational

Series), *Octopus* (Logan House, 2008, Winner of the Holland Prize), *Teaching Poetry Writing: A Five-Canon Approach* (Multilingual Matters LTD., 2007, New Writing Viewpoints Series), and *My Life as a Minor Character* (Pecan Grove, 2005, winner of national chapbook contest).

Christina Hutchins' poems appear in *Alehouse, Antioch Review, Beloit Poetry Journal, Denver Quarterly, The Missouri Review, The New Republic, Oberon, Prairie Schooner, Salmagundi*, and *The Southern Review*. She won the 2009-2010 *Missouri Review* Prize for Poetry. Sixteen Rivers Press will publish her book *The Stranger Dissolves* in 2011. She teaches poetry, poetics, and the philosophy of Alfred North Whitehead at Pacific School of Religion in Berkeley and is Poet Laureate of Albany, California.

Melissa Hotchkiss's first book of poems, *Storm Damage*, was published by Tupelo Press. Her poems and prose have appeared in numerous publications such as *The American Poetry Review, Green Mountains Review, Free Inquiry, LIT, Upstairs at Duroc* and the anthology *Poets for Palestine*. Melissa is one of the founding editors at Barrow Street Press, which has been producing the poetry journal *Barrow Street* for 12 years and books for eight years. She teaches at the Ocean State Summer Writing Conference at the University of Rhode Island, Kingston in the summers. Melissa lives in New York City.

Dorine Jennette is the author of *Urchin to Follow* (The National Poetry Review Press, 2010). Her poems, essays, and reviews have appeared in publications such as *Verse Daily, the Journal, Ninth Letter, Puerto del Sol, the New Orleans Review*, and the *Georgia Review*. Originally from Seattle, she earned her MFA from New Mexico State University and her PhD from the University of Georgia. She lives in Davis, California.

Stacy Kidd is completing a PhD in English at the University of Utah. Her poems have appeared in Boston Review, Columbia, Eleven Eleven, The Iowa Review, and WITNESS, among others. Her chapbooks About Birds and A man in a boat in the summer are forthcoming from Dancing Girl and Beard of Bees. She is founder and editor of the new online journal intersection(s), which launches this winter and is found here: intersectionsjournal.org.

Andrew McFadyen-Ketchum has recent or forthcoming poems, interviews, and reviews in *The Missouri Review, Hayden's Ferry Review, Sou'wester, The Spoon River Poetry Review, Copper Nickel, Rattle, Glimmer Train, Third Coast, The Southern Indiana Review, CENTER, Grist, Cold Mountain Review, The Cortland Review*, and *The Crab Orchard Review*, among others. He is the Founder and Editor of PoemoftheWeek.org, an online forum of Contemporary American Poetry, original and previously-published interviews, essays, and reviews.

J. Morris has published fiction and poetry in many literary magazines in the U.S. and Great Britain, including *The Southern Review, Missouri Review, Five Points, Subtropics, Prairie Schooner*, and *Fulcrum*. His work has been nominated for a Pushcart Prize and reprinted in *Twentieth Century Literary Criticism*. A chapbook, *The Musician, Approaching Sleep*, appeared in 2006 from Dos Madres Press.

Marcus Myers lives in Kansas City, Missouri, where he teaches gifted & talented middle school students and fathers a sassy toddler named Audrey. His writing has appeared in or is forthcoming from *H_NGM_N, Main Street Rag, Mid-American Review, New Zoo Poetry Review, Plainspoke, Pleiades*, and *Tar River Poetry*.

A Brooklyn New York native, **Jessica Piazza** is currently pursuing a PhD in Literature and Creative Writing at USC. Her poems have appeared or are forthcoming in *Agni, Mid-American Review, 32 Poems, Rattle*, and *Forklift Ohio*, among other places.

Melissa Studdard is a contributing editor for both *Tiferet* and *The Criterion* and a Reviewer at Large for *The National Poetry Review*. Her work has appeared in numerous journals, including *Boulevard, Connecticut Review, Gradiva, Dash*, and *Chelsea*. She holds an MFA from Sarah Lawrence College and teaches English and Creative Writing for Lone Star College-Tomball.

Angela Vogel's poems appear in *Best New Poets 2008, Verse Daily, Gulf Coast, Barn Owl Review, Cimarron Review, The Journal, The Southeast Review, Barrow Street, POOL, Southern Poetry Review, The American Poetry Journal*, etc. and are scheduled to appear in *Sou'wester*. Awards include the 2008 Southeast Review Poetry Prize, a Maryland State poetry fellowship, two Pushcart Prize nominations, and a residency at the Mary Anderson Center for the Arts. Her chapbook, *Social Smile*, is available from Finishing Line Press.

Sidney Wade has published five collections of poems, the most recent of which is *Stroke (*Persea Books, 2008). Her poems and translations have appeared in a wide variety of journals, including *Poetry, The New Yorker, Grand Street, Paris Review, The New Republic, The Gettysburg Review, Two Lines*, and *The Kenyon Review*, among others. She has taught at the University of Florida in the Creative Writing Program since 1993 and is the poetry editor of the literary journal *Subtropics*.

William D. Waltz is the author of *Zoo Music*. His poems have recently appeared in *Court Green, Denver Quarterly, jubilat*, and *Washington Square*. He lives in Saint Paul, Minnesota with his wife and children. He is the founder and editor of *Conduit*.

Ulla Gmeiner, Fine Artist

Paintings
mixed media, acrylics, oils

Graphics
digital collage, photocollage, mixed media collage

Objects
assemblage, landart, sculpture, installation

www.ullagmeiner.com

TIMOTHY MARTIN

Timothy Martin is a classically trained fine artist whose paintings have enchanted audiences worldwide.

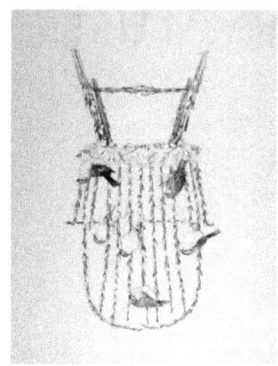

Chairs that charm, phantasmagorical furniture, musical instruments that mesmerize, tantalizing teapots ... enter the imagination of Timothy Martin and prepare to be entranced.

Visit www.timothymartin.com and browse his gallery of hundreds of works, each one as beguiling as the next. Original and limited editions, posters, cards, puzzles and gifts.

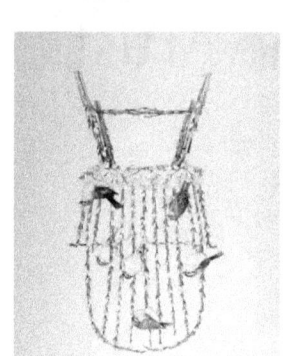

Find out why Timothy Martin has been embraced by some of the most prestigious names in the world.

TIMOTHY MARTIN FINE ART
www.timothymartin.com

distinction ~ *innovation* ~ *joie de vivre*

The National Poetry Review

Offers **The Annie Finch Prize for Poetry.** All entries will be considered by the editor for publication. Submit up to three unpublished, uncommitted poems (10 pages maximum per group of three poems), cover letter with bio and contact information. Results will be posted on the web.

Fee $15.00.   *   Postmark deadline: 4/30/11. Personal checks only, please; NO money orders. Please visit the website for detailed instructions: www.nationalpoetryreview.com

C. J. Sage, TNPR, Post Office Box 2080, Aptos, California 95001-2080

The winner will receive $300 plus publication in The National Poetry Review.

Simultaneous submissions are acceptable, but if the work is selected by TNPR for the prize or for publication, it must be withdrawn from elsewhere unless you have withdrawn it from us two weeks before our acceptance. Multiple submissions are acceptable with a reading fee for each group of three poems. Page limit per group: 10

Please note that close friends, relatives, and students of the judge or the editor are not eligible for the prize. The judge will be asked to send back to TNPR's editor any poem that s/he recognizes; should this happen, the entrant's fee will be refunded.

The National Poetry Review is a non-profit organization.

www.nationalpoetryreview.com

The 2011 **APJ** Book Prize

2010 winner was **Quinn Latimer's** *Rumored Animals.*
2009 winner was **Mark Conway's** *Dreaming Man, Face Down.*
2008 winner was **Lisa Lewis's** *Burned House with Swimming Pool.*
2007 winner was **Matthew Guenettes's** *Sudden Anthem.*
The 2006 winner was **Theodore Worozbyt's** *The Dauber Wings.*

Who will be the author of the next book in this series? You?

The postmark deadline for entries to the 2011 *The American Poetry Journal* Book Prize is February 28, 2011. To enter, submit 50-65 paginated pages of poetry, table of contents, acknowledgments, bio, email address for results (No SASEs; manuscripts will be recycled), and a $25.00 non-refundable fee for each manuscript entered. The winner will receive $1000, publication, and 20 copies. All entries will be considered for publication. All styles are welcome. Multiple submissions are acceptable. Simultaneous submissions are acceptable, but if your manuscript is accepted for publication elsewhere you must notify The *American Poetry Journal* and/or Dream Horse Press immediately. Fees are non-refundable. Judging will be anonymous; writers' names should not appear anywhere on the manuscript. Please include your name and biographical information in a separate cover letter. Please be sure to include your email address. The winner is chosen by the editor of The *American Poetry Journal*, J.P. Dancing Bear. Close friends, students (former or present), and relatives of the the editor are NOT eligible for the contest; their entry fees will be refunded.

The *American Poetry Journal* Book Prize entries may be sent online or by sending them to:

The *American Poetry Journal* book prize
P. O. Box 2080
Aptos, California 95001-2080
Make checks payable to: Dream Horse Press

dreamhorsepress.com

"In'erstates." She holds a bachelor's degree from Scripps College in Literature and Studio Art. Please visit http://alicia.vandevorst.org/ for more information on her work.

MIKE WHITE is originally from Montreal and now lives in Salt Lake City. His poems have appeared in *Poetry, The New Republic, The Threepenny Review, The Iowa Review, The Antioch Review, Denver Quarterly*, as well as in a previous issue of *APJ*. A selection of his work was featured in the recent anthology *New Poets of the American West* (Many Voices Press).

Toronto. She can be reached through her Website: www.aleahsato.com.

TINA SCHUMANN's manuscript *As If* was awarded the Stephen Dunn Poetry Prize for 2010 and will see publication by Parlor City Press this year. Her work received honorable mention in *The Atlantic* Poetry Contest for 2008. She received an MFA from Pacific Lutheran University. Her work has appeared or is forthcomng in *The Cimarron Review, Crab Creek Review, Cranky Literary Journal, Harpur Palate, Ascent, Poetry International* and *PALABRA*. She lives in Seattle, Washington.

DANIELLE SELLERS is the author of *Bone Key Elegies* (Main Street Rag). Her poems have appeared in *River Styx, Subtropics, Smartish Pace, The Cimarron Review, Poet Lore, 32 Poems, Cold Mountain Review*, and elsewhere. Her reviews have appeared or are forthcoming in *The South Carolina Review, The Collagist*, and *Gently Read Literature*. She's the editor of *The Country Dog Review* and teaches at the University of Mississippi.

KATIE JEAN SHINKLE serves as Managing Editor for Del Sol Press, current Nonfiction Editor of *Black Warrior Review* and Assistant Poetry Editor for *DIAGRAM*. Her work has appeared or is forthcoming in *BlazeVOX, dislocate, PANK Magazine* and *Staccato Fiction*, among others

KEVIN SIMMONDS is a writer, musician and photographer originally from New Orleans. His writing has appeared in *Asia Literary Review, jubilat, Kyoto Journal, Poetry* and elsewhere. Most recently, he wrote the musical score for *Hope: Living and Loving with AIDS* which won a News and Documentary Emmy Award. In 2006, during his Fulbright fellowship to Singapore, he taught the first ever poetry workshops at Changi Prison. He lives in San Francisco.

JUDITH SKILLMAN's twelfth book *The Never* (Dream Horse Press, 2010). The recipient of an award from the Academy of American Poets for her book *Storm* (Blue Begonia Press, 1998), Skillman's work has appeared in *Poetry, FIELD, The Southern Review, The Midwest Quarterly, Seneca Review*, and numerous other journals and anthologies. A writer, educator, and editor, Skillman holds an M.A. in English Literature from University of Maryland, and lives in Kennydale, Washington.

ELEANOR SWANSON's work has appeared or is forthcoming in a number of publications including *The Missouri Review, The Denver Quarterly*, and *The Southern Review*. Her book, *A Thousand Bonds: Marie Curie and the Discovery of Radium*, won the 2003 Ruth Stevens Manuscript Competition (NFPS Press) and was a finalist for the Colorado Book Award. Her most recent poetry collection, *Trembling in the Bones*, was published in 2006 by Ghost Road Press. She teaches at Regis University in Denver.

MATT SUMMERS ' work has appeared in *The Notre Dame Review, Thieves Jargon, Rivet, The Santa Clara Review, Wilderness House Literary Review*, and *Issue*. Originally from the Pacific Northwest, he lives in Boston where he received his MFA from Emerson College.

DAVID THACKER's poems have appeared in *Margie, Nimrod, Rhino*, and *Blood Orange Review*. He teaches English at the University of Idaho in Moscow, where he lives with his wife and daughters.

ALICIA VANDEVORST is a poet and photographer who lives in Grass Valley, California. She has just completed her first manuscript, *The Honey Archives*. Earlier writing includes a libretto, *Birnam Wood*, and a long poem in four voices, honors. He has a website at www.troublewithhammers.com.

KEITH MONTESANO's first book, *Ghost Lights*, a finalist for the 2008 Orphic Prize, and was published by Dream Horse Press in 2010. Other poems have appeared or are forthcoming in *Hayden's Ferry Review*, *American Literary Review*, *Third Coast*, *River Styx*, *Crab Orchard Review*, *Sonora Review*, *Passages North*, and elsewhere. He currently lives with his wife in New York, where he is a PhD Candidate in English and Creative Writing at Binghamton University.

ALAN JUDE MOORE is from Dublin, Ireland. Two collections of poetry, *Black State Cars* (2004) & *Lost Republics* (2008), are published by Salmon Poetry. His third collection, *Strasbourg*, will be published, also by Salmon, in autumn 2010. His fiction has been twice short-listed for the Hennessy Literary Award for New Irish Writing. His website is http://www.alanjudemoore.com

JULIE L. MOORE is the author of *Slipping Out of Bloom* (WordTech Editions, 2010) and the chapbook, *Election Day* (Finishing Line Press, 2006). Moore is a Pushcart Prize nominee and recent recipient of the Rosine Offen Memorial Award from the Free Lunch Arts Alliance in Illinois, the Janet B. McCabe Poetry Prize from *Ruminate: Faith in Literature and Art*, and the Judson Jerome Poetry Scholarship from the Antioch Writers' Workshop. Moore has contributed poetry to *Alaska Quarterly Review*, *Atlanta Review*, *CALYX*, *Chautauqua Literary Review*, *Cimarron Review*, *Dogwood*, *The MacGuffin*, *The Southern Review*, *Sou'Wester*, and *Valparaiso Poetry Review*. Her website is www.julielmoore.com.

CHRISTIAN NAGLE's poems, stories, essays, interviews and translations in *The Paris Review*, *Esquire Japan* , *Southwest Review*, *Partisan Review*, *New England Review*, *Kyoto Journal*, *Measure*, *Antioch Review*, *TSRPR*, *PBQ*, *Cimarron Review*, *Connecticut Review*, *Gulf Coast* , *Phoebe*, *The Texas Review*, *The Florida Review*, *Quick Fiction*, and elsewhere. His first collection, *Flightbook*, will be coming out from Salmon Poetry (Ireland).

OCTAVIO QUINTANILLA's poems are forthcoming in *Alaska Quarterly Review*, *Concho River Review*, *Bateau*, *zaum*, *Chaffey Review*, *mythium*, *Eclipse*, *SLAB*, and elsewhere. He is ABD at the University of North Texas.

PHOEBE REEVES's first chapbook, *The Lobes and Petals of the Inanimate*, was released by Pecan Grove Press in fall 2009 and was nominated for a Pushcart Prize. Some of the journals her poems have recently appeared in, or are forthcoming in, include *The Tampa Review*, *DIAGRAM*, *Gertrude*, *Poet Lore*, and *Quarterly West*.

ARRA LYNN ROSS is the author of the book *Seedlip and Sweet Apple* (Milkweed Editions), and has published work in *Harper's Ferry*, *Spoon River Poetry Review*, *Beloit Poetry Journal*, *Alimentum*, and *Linebreak*. Her work has also appeared on *Verse Daily* and the Academy of American Poets' Poem-a-Day. She earned her PhD in creative writing from the University of Nebraska—Lincoln and teaches creative writing at Saginaw Valley State University in Michigan.

ALEAH SATO is the author of *Badlands, Stillborn Wilderness* (Pooka Press) and the forthcoming *Empire of Moths*. Her work has appeared in *Nthposition*, *Adirondack Review*, *juked*, *Blue Fifth Review*, *Shadowtrain*, *BlazeVox*, *The Furnace Review*, *The Argotist*, and *Eclectica*, among others. Her collaboration with photographer Elizabeth Siegfried was exhibited at the G+ Galleries in

KERRI FRENCH is a recipient of the Larry Franklin and Mei Kwong Fellowship from the Writers' Room of Boston. Her poetry has been featured on Sirius Satellite Radio and was selected for inclusion in *Best New Poets 2008*, edited by Mark Strand. She holds degrees from Boston University, UNC-Chapel Hill, and UNC-Greensboro, and her poetry has appeared in *The Southeast Review, Barrelhouse, Agenda, Brooklyn Review, Fugue, DIAGRAM, Natural Bridge*, and *Lumina*, among others.

JEANNINE HALL GAILEY's first book of poetry, *Becoming the Villainess*, was published by Steel Toe Books. Poems from the book were featured on NPR's *The Writer's Almanac* and on Verse Daily; two were included in 2007's *The Year's Best Fantasy and Horror*. Her poems have appeared or are upcoming in *The Iowa Review, Prairie Schooner and Ninth Letter*; her essays, reviews and interviews have appeared on *Poets & Writers* online, the Poetry Foundation web site, and in *The American Book Review*. She volunteers as an editorial consultant for *Crab Creek Review* and currently teaches at the MFA program at National University. Her second book, *She Returns to the Floating World*, will be published in 2011 by Kitsune Books.

WILLIAM F. HOLDEN lives, works and studies Russian language at Portland State University in Oregon. At the age of twenty, this is his first official publication.

LOIS P. JONES has been published in *Rose & Thorn, Tiferet, The California Quarterly, Kyoto Journal*, and other journals in the U.S. and abroad. She is co-founder of Word Walker Press and a documentarist of Argentina's wine industry. You can hear her as host of Poet's Cafe (Pacifica Radio) and co-producer of Moonday's monthly series at Village Books. She is Associate Poetry Editor of *Kyoto Journal*, a 2009 Pushcart nominee, and 2010 nominee for *Best New Poets*.

SANDRA KOHLER's third collection of poems, *Improbable Music*, is forthcoming in 2011 from Word Press. Her second collection, *The Ceremonies of Longing*, winner of the 2002 AWP Award Series in Poetry, was published by the University of Pittsburgh Press in November, 2003. An earlier volume, *The Country of Women*, was published in 1995 by Calyx Books. Her poems have appeared over the past thirty years in journals including *Prairie Schooner, the New Republic, Beloit Poetry Journal*, and *The Colorado Review*.

ÉIREANN LORSUNG is the author of *Music for Landing Planes By* (Milkweed Editions) and *Projet Linguistique* (forthcoming, Milkweed Editions). Her poems appear in *Prairie Schooner, Barrelhouse, Diode*, and *Crab Creek Review*; she also reviews for *Staple Magazine* (UK). The organizer of the Nottingham Poetry Series, she lives in Nottingham, UK.

RACHEL MCKIBBENS currently resides in upstate New York. Her poems and short stories have appeared in numerous journals and anthologies including *World Literature Today, Monkey Bicycle, Wicked Alice* and *Bowery Women: Poems*. She is a New York Foundation for the Arts poetry fellow and her first collection of poems, *Pink Elephant* (Cypher Books) was released in December, 2009.

MICHAEL MEYERHOFER's second book, *Blue Collar Eulogies*, was published by Steel Toe Books. His first, *Leaving Iowa*, won the Liam Rector First Book Award. He has also won the Marjorie J Wilson Best Poem Contest, the James Wright Award, and Laureate Prize, the Annie Finch Prize for Poetry, and other

Contributors

RALPH ANGEL is the author of four books of poetry, most recently *Exceptions and Melancholies* (2007 PEN USA Poetry Award), as well as a translation of the Federico García Lorca collection, *Poema del cante jondo / Poem of the Deep Song*. Both are available from Sarabande Books.

REBECCA ARONSON has poems recently or soon in *Quarterly West, Cream City Review*, and *Prairie Schooner*, among others. Her first book—*Creature, Creature*—won the Main-Traveled Roads poetry book contest and was published in 2007. She lives in New Mexico where she teaches writing, ogles the mountains, and attempts to garden.

REBECCA KINZIE BASTIAN has appeared in a number of journals, including as an honorable mention in the *Ellipsis* Prize, judged by Claudia Rankine; in *Kalliope*, as a finalist in the Sue Saniel Elkind Poetry Contest; and most recently in *Rhino, Coal Hill Review, Pax Americana* and *Pebble Lake Review*. Poems have also been accepted for publication in *Frost Writing*, a Swedish journal.

EMMA BOLDEN's chapbooks include *How to Recognize a Lady* (part of *Edge by Edge*, Toadlily Press), *The Mariner's Wife* (Finishing Line Press), and *The Sad Epistles* (Dancing Girl Press). She was a semi-finalist for the Perugia Press Book Prize and a finalist for the Cleveland State University Poetry Center's First Book Prize and for a Ruth Lily Fellowship.

LIA BROOKS' poetry has appeared in *Penumbra, South, Shadow Train, First Time, California Quarterly, Loch Raven Review* and various other print and online magazines and anthologies in the U.K. and the U.S. She was short-listed by Sheenagh Pugh for the New Leaf Short Poetry Prize in 2007 and her poetry has been part of two ekphrastic events in collaboration with painters in Indiana and California. Her work has recently appeared in a 200 years commemoration to Chopin, and is also forthcoming in *Autumn Sky Poetry*. She resides in Southampton, UK, with her partner and two sons.

JAMES CIHLAR is the author of the poetry book *Undoing* (Little Pear Press) and chapbook *Metaphysical Bailout* (Pudding House Press), and his poems have appeared or are forthcoming in *Mary, Rhino, Painted Bride Quarterly, Emprise Review, Prairie Schooner*, and *Verse Daily*. The Book Review Editor for *American Poetry Journal* and the Poetry Editor for *Referential Magazine*, he lives in St. Paul, Minnesota.

JOHN DEMING is co-editor of *Coldfront Magazine*. His poems have appeared in *Boston Review, Verse Daily, POOL, Parthenon West Review*, and elsewhere. He lives in New York City and teaches at Baruch College and LIM College.

MERYL DEPASQUALE lives in Minneapolis and teaches at the Loft Literary Center. She is a graduate of the MFA program at the University of Minnesota. Her work has appeared in *CT Review* and *Midway Journal* and she has received a grant from the Minnesota State Arts Board.

DAVID DOODY is a founding editor of *InDigest Magazine*. His writing has appeared in the *Huffington Post, the Minneapolis Star Tribune, Guernica Magazine*, and mnartists.org, among other places.

KATE HANSON FOSTER gained her MFA in Poetry at Bennington College, Vermont. Her most recent poetry has appeared or is forthcoming in *Pebble Lake Review, Hobble Creek Review, California Quarterly* and *KnockOut Magazine*. She lives and writes in Groton, Massachusetts.

the dock a long way off, the bow line gone.

This is the world we want to inhabit. Like Patricia Gray's tomato, we want to "do what [we're] made for": we want to be as succulent as the ripe fruits we eat; like Moira Egan's artichokes, we want to be "stripped bare right down to the heart"; we want to believe we are what we eat—that we are—like the humble pea—made of "small mists of sweetgrass, pineroot, peat, seawater, ancient stone" (Rod Jellema). Like Judy Neri, we too hunger for the light that

> tells of earth's bounty cultivated and savored,
> the wine poured, the second nature of talk
> and writing that inhabits the dust which every day
> must be moved in homage.

Edited by Grace Cavalieri, the Annapolis, Maryland, author of numerous poetry books and chapbooks and the host of "The Poet and the Poem," and translated by Sabine Pascarelli who lives in Tuscany, *The Poet's Cookbook* is a mouthwatering tribute to Italian cooking.

> What I wouldn't do
> when I'm Mrs. McCann's age—
> still stopping
>
> to breathe the pleasure
> of another new
> dawn.

In pieces such as this, Reese is not simply showing us a picture; he forces us to think beyond the present. It is in that propulsion forward when Reese is the most successful and his poems most interesting. In *ghost on 3rd* Jim Reese is at his best when he pushes his subjects to give him a little more than they would on their own.

THE POET'S COOKBOOK: RECIPES FROM TUSCANY
by Grace Cavelieri and Sabine Pascarelli. Bordighera Press, 2009. 6 x 9". 143 pages. $12.00. Paperback. ISBN-13: 978-1599540115

REVIEWED BY ARRA LYNN ROSS

Described on the cover as "Poems by 28 Italian and American Poets," this collection is perhaps more accurately described as a cookbook of recipes showcasing Tuscan food. Despite this slight problem with packaging, I did find both lovely pieces and mouth-watering recipes. The book is organized into sections, from Appetizers to Soups to the First Course, Second Course, Vegetables, Salads, and Deserts. Ten recipes are included in each section, followed by three to five poems that correspond in some way to the general sectional theme. The recipes themselves are simple and easy to make. I recommend trying the Tomato Soup with Bread, the Risotto with Saffron, the Rich Summer Vegetables and Asparagus alla Farnesina, the Cucumber Salad, the Chocolate-Wine Cake, or the Pears in Cream (with rum, six egg yolks, sugar, and a whole pint of whipping cream).

    Featured poets include Karren LaLonde Alenier, Cecily Angleton, David Budbill, Andrea Hollander Budy, Anne Caston, Jenny D'Angelo, Tina Daub, Moira Egan, Jean Emerson, Emily Ferrara, Nan Fry, Maria Mazziotti Gillan, Michael S. Glaser, Barbara Goldberg, Patricia Gray, Carole Wagner Greenwood, Rod Jellema, Diane Lockward, Calder Lowe, Judy Neri, Linda Pastan, Alexis Rotella, Carly Sachs, Vivian Shipley, Rose Solari, Christine Sostarich, Katherine Williams, and Ernie Wormwood.

    Reading through the poems, I find myself "held in hunger's pleasure swoon," as Emily Ferrara writes in her piece "Making Lasagna." It's easy to enter into the realm of delicious praise, to find panacea in the meld of sensuous words and food and memory, a kind of ecstatic drunkenness, like Christina Daub writes: "the river rising inside you,"

> till there you are, brim, half-bobbing
> with affection, laughter, half-drowning,
> kissing, saying, *yes, my darling, yes*

> are strewn across the yard.
> It's nine o'clock and, for two more hours,
> if Willow doesn't wake,
>
> this time is ours.
> The cool buzz of the baby monitor,
> the cheesy brats bursting on the grill,
> the gurgle and kiss.

The subtle rhyme of "art" and "yard" and the not-so-subtle rhyme of "hours" and "ours," along with the alliteration throughout ("glows," "glee," "gurgle"; "buzz," "baby," "brats bursting"; "Willow," "wake") make this scene poetic. It is a heartwarming and vivid scene, made more so by Reese's attention to craft rather than simply relying on family sentiment.

Other poems of family in the collection are less successful. "Would you mind reading this new poem?" appears to be exactly what the title implies—a poet asking his wife to read a new poem and the conversation that ensues. Thematically, the only thing of interest in this poem is when the speaker asks about a particular line in the "new poem," because the line shows up again in the final poem in this book ("Free those breasts and their veiny road maps"), giving us a glimpse of the poet's process.

Similarly, "At Three Years My Daughter Recites Her First Poem" is presumably just what the title says, perhaps a poem only a father could love:

> Dad. Look!
> I'm a stinky monkey
> hanging on the doorknob
> like a fart.

If in some poems Reese falls into the parental trap of bragging about the accomplishments of his children, in others he takes up the challenge of showing where family scenes and experiences can take us, while crafting the language to equal the beauty and intensity of the moment.

There are lighter moments in *ghost on 3rd*, as well. In "The Woman Who Wishes to Remain Anonymous Bakes a Cherry Pie" we are reminded of the fact that family and friends of writers live in constant worry that they will show up in a poem or story. Therefore, we read about Reece's mother as "The Woman Who Wishes to Remain Anonymous." Funnier still in this poem, the pie they are eating was made from cherries his mother froze in 1978, leading his stepfather to say, "We've been eating it and haven't got sick yet." Reese again lightens things up when, in "Poetry Reading—Tonite," he describes an awkward poetry reading with poets who seem to be more into the *idea* of being a poet than concerned with the actual quality of their poetry: "The pale poet with his receding hairline; / who is still hanging onto his Pearl Jam / ponytail," and "His major artistic influence—Mr. / Magoo and trail mix, which keeps him regular."

And then there are poems that succeed as observational poems, such as "The Grass Alley," in when Reese describes an elderly neighbor smelling her flowers:

him, at thirty-five years old, still unable to get the murderer out of his head. As a father Reese worries about a world in which he has to ask, as in "The Metal Detector,"

> As I tuck her into bed tonight, I wonder:
> will monsters with canes
> and bloody shirts interrupt what should be
> precious thoughts of this world we live in?

Such experiences make it hard to know why someone would place himself among the people who have been convicted of crimes like the one that took place in Reese's childhood neighborhood and have left him with a gnawing fear for his daughters' well being. In one of the best poems in this collection, however, Reese reveals a gift for empathy. "Jesus Christ Pose" describes a prisoner "In a theatre practicum in San Quentin":

> You raise your hands, palms up.
> head dangling down,
> your Jesus Christ pose.
>
> You begin to stand on one foot.
> ...
> *Every morning, you say, after my foster father left for work,*
> *she made me stand in the corner like this.*

Reese concludes with such dry certainty it made me flinch in recognition and agreement: "And now I understand why / some of you are here."

"Jesus Christ Pose" suggests an acquired understanding of why some heinous crimes happen. Through the poet's work with the people who commit them, he is forced to look closer and closer at their human faces, as in "Vernon is Taking the Dirty Dog Home":

> I've been instructed never to get too close
> to any inmate. But I'm your teacher, and I'm afraid that's just not
> possible. Tonight, like most nights,
> I carry you home with me.

Caught in the enigma of how humans can both love and hurt, Reese is torn between his constant drive to protect his daughters ("You want to ride your bike around the block— / by yourself") and his desire to help the sort of people whose actions have made the world a dangerous place in which his daughters need protecting.

In the poems more fully given over to the joys and frustrations of fatherhood, Reese is most successful when he makes the language and the scene beautiful or intense for the reader, as in *"How do you like my M's?"*:

> The sidewalk art
> glows with glee.
> My daughter's sand box toys

supposing a kind of eternal life that can exist in literature, or in literature as it is a representation of the imagined, and so eternal, life. Next, German philosopher Walter Benjamin—who killed himself with morphine while on the run from Nazis in 1940—is brought into the mix. The speaker notes that his own grandfather was named after Benjamin, and his own father was named after Celan. The poem moves like a dreamscape; it is repetitive and disjointed, but all the while alluring, a mind deep inside its own twisted caves. Williams works to a conclusion that refuses to undermine or understand the human potential for vileness, but that provides release as well:

> So, gulp down the morphine quickly, because of your shame for the humans,
> what humans can do to each other. Benjamin, grandfather, Walter;
> Paul, father, Celan: all the names that ever existed wiped out in shame.
>
> Celan on his bridge. Rashkolnikov muttering Dostoevsky under his breath.
> Jew on bridge. Rashkolnikov-Dostoevsky still in my breath. Under my breath.
> Black milk of daybreak. *Aschenes Haar*. Antschel-Celan. Ash. Breath.

"Jew on Bridge," along with "Apes," "Assumptions," and a broad variety of (anti-) war poems, acknowledges human brutality and our limp justifications for that brutality. Yet as this poem concludes *Wait*, there is something ethereal in its final syllable, "breath." It recalls a passage from the book's penultimate poem, "The Foundation": "Watch me, I'm running, watch me, I'm dancing, I'm air." And later: "Watch me again now, because I'm not alone in my dancing, / my being air, I'm with my poets, my Rilke, my Yeats . . ." He goes on to name twenty-two more poets, each marked with "my." The poet accesses salvation in his own mind by living deep inside it, even beyond it.

Earlier this year, Williams published a book about Walt Whitman, who concludes his most famous poem by telling his readers, "If you want me again look for me under your bootsoles." Williams finds not only Whitman there, but everyone he's ever read and admired, living or dead. When he resists easy sentimentality—when he resists finality, or clear understanding—he shows that he is fixing to join them. Or has joined them already.

GHOST ON 3RD
by Jim Reese. NYQ Books, 2010. 88 pages. 6 x 9". $14.95. ISBN-13: 978-1935520177

Reviewed by David Doody

In *ghost on 3rd*, Jim Reese's second book, poems of fatherhood live side by side with poems about working with prisoners, in an unlikely juxtaposition somewhat eerily mediated by the poet's childhood memory of murder in his small town.

In addition to being an Assistant Professor of English at Mount Marty College in South Dakota and Editor in Chief of *Paddlefish*, Reese has been the National Endowment for the Arts' Writer in Residence at the Yankton Federal Prison Camp since 2008.

In "Missing" we learn that the murders of two boys in Nebraska by a sexual predator took place in Reese's neighborhood when he was a child, leaving consciousness to the point of unconsciousness; he has a line on something, and the urge to question generates a sense of place and location. Questioning is hard, but it's real; we can live there.

Yet in a number of these poems, particularly in section 1 (of 4), he trusts himself too much. In "On the Metro," he makes eye contact with a young woman: "and then, as Gombrowicz puts it, she 'affirms herself physically,' that is, / becomes present in a way she hadn't been before." The speaker then "can't help but remark / her strong figure and very tan skin—(how literally golden young women can look at the end of summer)." When the train rocks, their arms touch, and she doesn't pull hers away, and the speaker regards that to be touched is to be "acknowledged, *known*."

Next comes the disclaimer: "I understand that in no way is she offering more than this, and in truth, I have no desire for more." The use of "in truth," as well as the set piece itself, might lead one to comment, *Oh, I think he does.* The significance of the scene—feeling "known" through touch, the notion that the girl "affirms herself physically"—is a result of the narrator's own imaginative impositions. Robert Bly's 1966 critique of Robert Lowell's *For the Union Dead* seems aptly applied here; Bly states that most of the poems in Lowell's book "are melodrama; the inner and outer worlds have split apart." Here we see the poet manipulating his environment to support a priori rather than inductive conclusions. The result for the reader in this case is a sense of disconnect or unease—a poet whose calling card is frankness and transparency has let his artifice show through.

The train incident in "On the Metro" leads to a boyhood memory: "a girl I'd mooned from afar, across the table in the library in school now." After rejecting the off-color sense of the term and mentally correcting the image, the reader likely mourns the poem's turn to sentiment. One could do worse than to channel grandfatherly, cornbread narratives, but Williams sometimes dips into schmaltz, with, occasionally, pathetic fallacy as a result: in "Light," memory is "steamed away / like the film of uncertain vapor," and in "Ponies," the ponies buck "like the brutes their genes must dream they still are." That vapor can be uncertain, that genes can dream, all seems a little fantastic. *Wait* could lose these and maybe a handful of other poems—"Thrush," "Wasp," and "Blackbird," to name a few—without losing much.

But there are extraordinary poems in here, too, and they tend to develop from Williams pursuing one of two kinds of mania: the horrific emptiness of war and human wickedness, and the corrective ecstasy of swimming in the skies with his favorite poets and philosophers. He blends both conceits in the book's best poem—truly, one of Williams' best to date—"Jew on Bridge." Williams recalls a scene from *Crime and Punishment* in which Rashkolnikov sees precisely what the title indicates, and splices it with the suicide of German-speaking Romanian and Jewish poet Paul Celan, who leapt from a bridge in 1970:

> He stood on the bridge over the Seine, looked into the black milk of dying,
> Jew on bridge, and hauled himself over the rail. *Dein aschenes Haar*....
> Dostoevsky's Jew, though, is still there. On page something or other.

Here, Williams borrows Celan's most famous image—black milk—before

Wait

by C. K. Williams. Farrar, Straus & Giroux, 2010. 6 x 9". 144 pages. Hardcover. $25.00. ISBN-13: 978-0374285913

Reviewed by John Deming

Sometimes C. K. Williams jumps to conclusions. But he'd be the first to tell you that. "Rash," a poem from his new book *Wait*, begins:

> Ten times an hour, it feels like, I arrive in my brooding,
> my fretting, my grumbling, at enormous generalizations,
> ideations, intellections, speculations, which before
> they're even wholly here I know I'll soon disprove.

The lines imply that even when reason dictates a plausible course, one can never arrive at any definitive truth about anything. Yet brainwork, however futile, is central to Williams, and therein lies his central problem: a constant urge to be axiomatic rubs against an inevitable need to destroy all axioms. When he fights off rigid conclusions, he can be electric; when he doesn't, he winds up speaking—sometimes meekly, sometimes with high melodrama—from a position of assumed authority.

In *Wait*, Williams joins the recent prolific and productive cadre of modern masters contemplating mortality. This septuagenarian poet, whose previous volume was the critically acclaimed *Collected Poems*, has characteristically relied on his own associations—I experience *this*, which makes me think of *that*, which is why I'm telling you *this*, which may or may not mean *that*—to negotiate his way to the end of a poem. This method is exercised in many of the poems in *Wait*.

Frequently, poems in *Wait* open with a reference to something the speaker has read. He begins "Marina" with, "As I'm reading Tsvetaeva's essays," then supplies a quote from an essay, then continues: "a tiny insect I don't recognize / is making its way across my table." "Brain," on the other hand, is wholly abstract:

> I was traversing the maze of my brain: corridors, corners, strange narrow caverns, dead-ends.
> Then all at once my being like this in my brain, this sense of being my brain, became unbearable to me.
>
> I began to wonder in dismay if the conclusion I'd long ago come to that there can be nothing
> that might be reasonably be postulated as the soul apart from body and mind was entirely valid.

Deciding for certain that the soul is a fiction is as limiting as deciding for certain that the soul is real. Williams habitually contests assumptions. If doing so yields any kind of answer, that answer will in turn become an assumption that must be contested. He is always reasoning his way to the next square, and is at his best when he's so deep inside his own mind that he seems to know nothing at all. It's lively and inventive juxtapositions. The text's movement is at turns whimsical and startling, and frequently hilarious. Personality brims in these transitions:

> I could always escape by mooning away about my fabulous future as a movie star. Then I suddenly realized—I don't have any make-up! I was sure that the pounding of my heart could be heard all over the theatre.

In step with the protagonist, the gaps between sentences contain an electric mixture of tension and bravado. This effect owes part of its success to the variety of tools in the kit. The prose of *By Myself* follows Simone de Beauvoir with Drew Barrymore, sets Ronald Regan alongside The Rock, nuzzles Joan Rivers and Ginger Rogers, erases the space between Dolly Parton and The Duchess of Devonshire. The reader gets a one-line date with Miles Davis, Helen Keller, Paris Hilton, and countless others.

Additionally, *By Myself* uses sentence-order to joke with its collaborators and its genre. After describing a memorable night at the Academy Awards and his dinner partner, the protagonist rapidly shifts gears:

> But the last time I looked in a mirror, I bore little or no resemblance to Shelley Winters and this is not going to be another "tell-all" autobiography. Through a glass darkly I saw Marlon sitting next to me and said, "Hi," then realized the only place I wanted to go was to the ladies' room. That was probably my greatest moment in pictures—I felt I had really passed the test.

The flirtation between telling and not telling takes on a new shade when a reader flips to the sources section and sees that the line about Brando comes from Shelley Winter's *Shelley: Also Known as Shirley*. The text's hybrid identification—fiction, memoir, found poem—allows for critique of tell-all autobiographies while also blowing them a big kiss. The most productive moments involve friction between reticence and performance mixed with a heightened consciousness of form:

> The journey into addiction has been described so often by so many people in recent years that I don't believe a blow-by-blow account of my particular path would serve any useful purpose. Everybody knows I like buttercream frosting on birthday cake. I was sunk.

Buttercream frosting is one of those unpredictable details that keeps the reader guessing and solves the problem of how to describe an already overplayed experience. The combination of particularity and mystery in this metaphor provides a way for the protagonist to distinguish himself while also representing all celebrities. He slips out of definitive categories of ethnicity, gender, and socioeconomics and doesn't need to reveal what he's been up to.

An individual driven to perform before others craves a state of singularity through distinction, as well as community through recognition. As the protagonist admits, "I didn't want to be by myself in the Hollywood Hills." Happily the text is well-populated. And while Powell and Trinidad's selections usually involve a lot of tongue-in-cheek, the narrative closes with a touching couplet one-half Alice B. Toklas and one-half Gertrude Stein. The chief joy in *By Myself* is that one never is.

Although Woloch's poems rely on specific locations, she transforms images (even the seemingly familiar) like a traveler moving through the world, where one image melts into another and returns as something luminous and new.

If there is one place in which the poet-voice finds refuge as a stillness, rather than refuge in movement, that place is Carpathia, for which the book is named, and which bears the longest note in the notes section. It's not surprising that Woloch mentions that the word for that mountainous region of Eastern Europe may come from the Indo-European word *kwerp*, which means "to turn, to change." It's also telling that Carpathia is where her father's people came from, and was a place of imagination rather than reality for much of her life. In "Postcard to Myself from the Lower Carpathians, Spring," Woloch manages to show both rest and movement happening simultaneously in a room full of white moths: "I knew, as soon as soon as I switched off the lamp, that the air would go pale with their fluttering. I knew, in my sleep, one might light on my arm, on my cheek, in my hair, without waking me."

She continues, "What I learned about gentleness then. What I learned to be gently less wary of." And here, in the way she subtly shifts the words—from "gentleness" to "gently less"—we see the gift that Carpathia, the place, the poem, the book, offers: the gentle turn "whose one white note is feast enough," for the invisible "beloved, all bright tenderness."

BY MYSELF: AN AUTOBIOGRAPHY
by D. A. Powell and David Trinidad. Turtle Point Press, 2009. 52 pages. 5 x 7.75". $9.00. ISBN-13: 978-1933527291

REVIEWED BY MERYL DEPASQUALE

When two poets write a fictional memoir composed entirely of lines from other memoirs, we know we're in for a playful pageant. When those two poets also happen to be D. A. Powell, Kingsley Tufts Award winner for *Chronic*, and David Trinidad, author of *The Late Show* and co-founder of the journal *Court Green*, who title their mutual endeavor *By Myself*, the project reaches the heights of parody. This mischievous chapbook eschews solitary artistic process in favor of collaboration, not only between Trinidad and Powell but also with a colorful cast of stars from the screen and stage, musicians, writers, public figures, and more than one heiress.

The text's collective generation allows for an interesting conversation about celebrity narratives; these sundry sentences catalog the quirky and cliché similarities found along the pathways to fame and stardom. The unnamed protagonist has humble beginnings and big dreams, a struggling artist period followed by his eventual break out, and problems with the tabloids, addiction, and his health. He has bones to pick, confessions he'll reveal and others he'll withhold, and finally he'll close with a picture of personal fulfillment and cozy domesticity. But the details that populate *By Myself* are anything but predictable and contain enough winking and innuendo to keep a reader fully absorbed.

The sentence is the performative unit in this work, and for this reason Powell and Trinidad don't aim for smooth combinations. Instead they select

The twelve prose poem "postcards" sprinkled liberally throughout the book also create sustaining tension. The nature of the postcard itself implies both movement and stillness, as well as the invocation of a beloved whom a writer addresses. Woloch's postcard poems are written to particular people who were with the poet in particular places and times, or they address herself, or they are from a dream at the edge of the sea, or from a long-dead writer's bed, etc. These postcards highlight the strange relationship between memory and the past— as if one could send a postcard to that long ago world, as if it still exists, as if that person, as they existed in that long ago moment, also still exists, changed, unchanged, "thorn and bud." At the same time that the postcard is in motion toward the past, it holds the present (or a present, even if that present existed in the past), which it sends into someone's near future. In essence, time and place are motion, like "that sky of a road."

Woloch's focus on time drives her fast-paced prose poem "Be Always Late," in which motion is a way of life, a way of entering the dishevelment of life through desire. The poem relies on the accrual of images and sounds to build a hurried and hopeful pace: the bridge, the silvery river, the church bells, the panting clouds, the wind at the nape of the neck, the heart clicking, the turning past the poor little park with its late little flowers, disheveled little flames, one's "shadow flaring out behind," always running / half-running "because somewhere someone waits. Because somewhere one has already arrived and will never rush past this again." The end of the poem plays with time-specific words and alliteration to show how one easily one time morphs into another: "Now and ever. Not never: late."

More evocative than Woloch's way of transforming time, though, is the way in which she transforms images. They are more than metaphors for something else—her images are themselves rich and surprising, and yet, they morph to create a landscape larger than reason, a bouquet of images that are in the very act of transforming, a transformation based more on accrual and change of position than on change of shape. This is particularly evident in the poem that introduces section II: "Why I Believed, as a Child, That People Had Sex in Bathrooms," which makes a surprising turn from the humorous title to look at how her parents loved each other, transforming our understanding of the bathroom door, the devil, sex, her parent's bed, her mother's dark hair, and the bathroom sink in surprising and tender ways as the poem unfolds, which can only be hinted at in the last stanza:

> how young they were—my mother
> soaping my father's back; her dark hair
> slipping out of its pins. . . .
> Because what was sex, after that? I didn't know
> he would ever die, this god in a body, strong as a god,
> or that she would one day hang her head
> over the bathroom sink to weep. I was a child,
> only one of their children. Love was clean.
> Babies came from singing. The devil was wood
> and had no eyes.

The poems in Celia Woloch's fourth collection draw the bucket from the deep well where the waters of grief and joy are inextricably mingled, drink deeply, then pass the weathered ladle to us. Composed of three sections, the book travels across landscapes in America and Europe, in dreams and in memories, to build a world where love does not fade, nor disappear with death, but endures, transformed, in our invisible spirit. Woloch has clearly been saving her "extravagancies of the heart, secretly (Rilke)," and in her carefully chosen words, she builds—from the bones of memory—an open field where she can hear her "own dead in the high / grass whispering, / beloved, beloved, beloved."

The collection moves like a serpentine river, doubling back on territory already covered, coursing past several bends, still "almost near enough to touch." The poems enact the accrual of experience by holding both the "shattered and shimmering"; yet, they go a step beyond, reaching back into the land of memory "to save what can still be saved of the girl who believed." Woloch's poems "love in reverse," infused with the tenderness craved by our former selves who were overtaken with the longing, "almost like rage, . . . to wreck ourselves on the world." Woloch gives her subjects that tenderness—like the light of dusk after we have "failed and failed at love," when "then" becomes the location in consciousness where "the Earth was a real place" and "the house in the meadow was lit from within by a child."

Woloch returns again and again to her father's last days and how he now surprises her after his death in the appearance of an old man driving a truck, or any stooped man just barely able to walk. In the first stanza of her poem "Mistake," Woloch uses line breaks and syntax, anaphora and repetition to transform images and objects, which become themselves even as they are more than themselves, and more than mere symbols:

> Near the end, he thought he saw death
> near the door where his dark robe hung.
> But it was only his robe in the dark.
> It was only the door. It was only his death
> come for him, and near.

The tone is at once both humble and awed, threaded with the knowledge of loss and "surrender." Placed immediately after a poem about her father's last fever, the poem "Brasov, 1989" displays this linkage clearly. Set in communist Romania, the poem becomes the landscape of the daughter's own internal grief—as if she were the women, broken, starved, waiting in line to confess—unexpectedly bathed in the light—"golden, warm, diffuse, / as if all sins, once confessed, or desires . . . could be left at the feet of a wooden saint / with a whisper, a kiss, a prayer for forgiveness: / Because we've been broken. Because we've obeyed." This last line shows the tautness and tension Woloch explores throughout the collection—evident also in the epigram by H.D. to the section section of the book: "to sing love / Love must first shatter us." Woloch's work surrenders itself to the inevitable breakage of loss that allows one to love fully, even if it is loving in reverse, in words.

We can only imagine the strength of character demanded by this subject, which requires the speaker not only to candidly divulge family secrets, but to imagine the horrors of her life in detail, to color her dead on the page. In "Heaven," Bachmann imagines her sister's abandoned half-naked body near a railroad:

> The lighting is soft, midmorning, hazy enough to blur
> the details, so we can fill them in any way we like.
>
> Say, a brunette, barely legal, hidden.
> From here, it looks like she's speechless.

This poem is striking for many reasons, not the least of which is that the speaker tells the story from all sides. Among others, she fully inhabits the mind of the killer. If detectives claim that is the way a mystery may be solved, for the reader, it's the way the horror of this history will be fully felt.
This collection's lack of sentimentality, self-pity, and hero-worship is admirable.

If the poems are variations on the elegy, they are phrased in startlingly objective terms. No unsubstantiated claims are made about the sister. We are not left with the impression that she was a god or a saint. Instead, we understand her fragility and humanity.
If in the body of the book we may not always have a clear sense of the character of the victim in life, then toward the end of the book the speaker provides a few lasting images that suggest what the young sisters were like together. In "Glorious Mystery," the speaker looks from above at two kids "addicted to glass" in the alley below her apartment. She says,

> one climbs the wall
> between the dumpster and the escape.
> The other clubs her fist into her thigh, sparking
> her cigarette. They're no angels but they're trying.

This image could serve as a metaphor for the sisters: the murdered one escapes into memory, while the other inflicts pain on herself in living history, trying to restore feeling, to create fire.

Reading this book, I am reminded of Pablo Neruda's advice given in his short essay, "Toward an Impure Poetry." He says poetry should be "worn with the hand's obligations, as by acids, steeped in sweat and in smoke, smelling of lilies and urine, spattered diversely by the trades that we live by, inside the law or beyond it." Bachmann, indeed, gives us the lilies and urine, almost literally, the dead and the beauty of the dead. Artfully constructed and classically mediated, this poet's first book also marks the depth of human grief and mourning. There can't possibly be anywhere for her to go but up from here.

CARPATHIA
by Cecilia Woloch. BOA Editions, 2009. 96 pages. 9.5 x 5.9" $16.00. Paperback. ISBN-13: 978-1934414262.

REVIEWED BY ARRA LYNN ROSS

Temper

by Beth Bachmann. University of Pittsburgh Press, 2009. 80 pages. 6 x 8.5".
$14.95. Paperback. ISBN-13: 978-0822960409

Reviewed by Danielle Sellers

In her first collection, *Temper*, Beth Bachmann walks the line between full disclosure and self-preservation. There's mystery, but the speaker has only clues, no definitive proof. What is not a secret in this collection is that Bachmann's older sister was murdered at age eighteen, and she approaches this subject in her book in mythic, imaginative, and investigative modes. The girls' father is a suspect. He is the mystery to the speaker, one that she tries to solve through various poems that act as plot-diagrams. The titular and first poem in the collection alludes to a mystery that is about to unfold: "Some things are damned to erupt like wildfire." And indeed, the second poem in the collection sets the blaze:

> Move closer. I want to tell you a story. It has its blood knots, its changing water,
> the usual lures: family, violence, a margin left bare for interpretive remark.

While there are a lot of blank margins left for the reader to interpret, there is nothing usual about the narrative the poems in this collection need to tell. Although murder is an unfortunate reality, rarely is a victim's family able to render the story in a way that is buoyant, air-filled, while honoring the loss. Bachmann is skilled at bruising the reader with the lightest touch, giving us details, then pulling away. In "First Mystery of My Sister," we are given the sort of glimpse we may assume obsessive readers of murder mysteries crave:

> Overgrowth, long fingers
> of grass, the bud of a dull tattoo—what remains—
>
> her tagged body,
> the dog at dawn sniffing a green rose.

We see the figurative tug-of-war at play within the speaker's mind by the frenetic length of lines on the page. At times, her lines are long and juicy, then sparse, as in the poem "Erato":

> *swan or angel,*
>   something to do with the divine, the light
>
> always, bending back.
>   Or you might remember the way
>
> a girl's tongue razes ice or catches the root of the word
>
> *muse*: an open mouth,
>   a muzzle.

Often, it's as if she's catching herself divulging a truth, then reining her emotion in.

from that world; just the opposite, in fact. Their play with language, with reference, and with context forms a glossy, sometimes sparkling surface through which mourning (for individual losses, but also for the destructive power of human beings) comes crashing—delicately, but no less destructively for that—as in "Bad Days," where a desolate narrator faces the fact that despite the beauty humans have made, despite "Dickinson, Bishop, Szymborska," in the end "music makes it easier to kill, easier to lie / easier to believe lies."

And so, when Bryan commands herself to "go in awe / of the universe, more in awe / than in fear" ("Essential"), she writes that command in the context of a book that reminds us that by the time we understand how things work they are over, that our understanding (especially of our own powers of destruction) is limited, and that the universe is larger and more powerful than we can imagine. That, in fact, we ourselves are more complex and unknowable than we can imagine. This is the detachment I'm talking about; not that Bryan's poems don't love the world (they do; take a look at the inventive and attentive wordplay in "Bass / Bass", for example) but in the end they know that "whatever we are is too / slippery to get a grip on" ("Soup"). It's the long view from space that sees the "universe / we live in, ninety-nine / percent dark" coupled with the voice of the "human brain / with its big bright eyes" ("Charming Quarks") which grasps its scale and its impermanence but hopes "there's a way / to love this life to distraction / without hating it for going on / without me" ("Die Happy").

The poems in *Sharp Stars* speak clearly because that's the best chance they have, in their universe, of transmitting properly. They reach out across distances in hopes of touching someone. Their longing and their speech, like music, "[require] / the loved one's absence" ("Proust's Jukebox"), and in this sense absence forms the core of the book, which is about beginnings in some ways but is much more about what happens once those beginnings are over and the rest of time sets in. Music—the music of poems in a world that lacked them before they were written, the music of the stars, Glenn Gould's fingers on the piano—comes out of the darkness, the silence that prompts speech, poetry, meaning in the first place. And the human noise points back to the ones who make it, to "mere mortals with sweaty / palms and opposable thumbs" ("Glenn Gould Humming"), who are, after all is said and done, both body and soul. The makers and the made-for. Alpha and Omega of our thinking and feeling.

After all, it is the human universe in which Bryan's poems take place, a universe that could only ever happen in terms that its creators could understand, in which even the terms of the unknown take place in our thought and language and music. The value of the human in this book's universe is the value of the power to create meaning—which, the poems acknowledge, is neither complete nor an unmitigated good. After Adam names the world (and thereby calls it into being for himself) in "Saying Things," he finds himself liking best "his earliest memories, / before he could hear himself / think, before all the razzle-dazzle." Sharon Bryan's poems are sharp-edged, sparkling, dangerous, mournful, occasionally celebratory—if this is what the razzle-dazzle of naming opens up, I'll take it and whatever accompanies it.

Reviewed by Éireann Lorsung

Way back, but no, *way* back, before the beginning of everything, depending on who you are and what you believe, there was the word. In Sharon Bryan's intelligent and crystalline, occasionally funny, often clever *Sharp Stars*, before even the word (if a division can be made), there is music: the lyrics of Bob Dylan; a big band warming up. Sound, music, speech, meaning, word: a human noise permeates *Sharp Stars*, thematic in both the literary and musical senses, being both what the poems treat and the repeated element that draws them together and makes sense from them. Music here embodies desire: it is "desire to be / in motion, waves of longing" ("Big Band Theory"), the desire at a beginning or at a loss that causes—simply *causes*. In Bryan's poems, this desire makes the universe explode from nothing (from "little flashes / of light, glints of brass") and it assures the beauty, and therefore the value, of that universe.

The universe of this book is beautiful in its enormity and unknowability, as well as in and through the patterns Bryan's human subjects create in order to understand it. Musicians, writers, scientists, and (for example) the makers of eau-de-vie all participate in this creation, although what Bryan's poems seem to acknowledge in their totality is that any understanding we have is partial, transient. Our noises have an expiration date. But the poems' concern with transmission—a transmission whose metaphor is the journey of light across vast distance—means that although one speaker says (and we believe her) that "I started wanting / to get on with my life, but I was afraid // to look away from something rare, something / I might never see again" ("Bluebird of Happiness"), the transmission continues beyond our expectations, our control, and our lifetimes. See, for example, the experience of tasting Framboise in "Eau de Vie": "in that one taste / was the history // of the universe that had made it / possible, not left // behind but transformed, translated / carried over." The making of beautiful things in the face of our certain deaths is "part of the universe / passing through us like a wave— / a kind of kinship, a kind of love" ("Stardust").

Bryan's patterned and constellated universe, despite its beauty, has very little of ease for its inhabitants, whose failing bodies burn, tremble, are lonely, forget, grieve, misspeak, and die. Even in poems about sorrow ("Erasures," "Welling," "Careless"), however, Bryan's poems try to *make sense*, order things, find a grammar for loss that would include it in the composition of the daily. And the tone caught this reader unaware—as, for instance, in "Die Happy," where the musing, conversational voice gives way, just after a thoughtful interrogation of what it could mean to die happy in the first place, to the final, stunning image, which clinches the poem's wondering without making either redundant:

> as if just before an avalanche
> rolled over him, a young man
> were caught in a friend's photo
>
> wild with joy in mountain snow.

Others of Bryan's poems also perform this tonal detachment from the world they love, which doesn't mean in the end that this reader felt disengaged that century—or anything— / together again?" ("The Camps"). The poem begins with Bernini's version, and right away we get that plainspoken language: "Who wouldn't feel a little squirmy, / standing in the line of fire. . . a growl, a squint focusing — O, everything on his target." The piece shifts when it leaps from the marble to the sculptor, and the twisted politics behind the commission — "the rage of an entire people burning behind" Bernini's eyes.

The second section displays more of Minczeski's real-world imagery, even humor, when he describes Michelangelo's sculpture: "Calm as a card shark sitting down / to the World Series of Poker . . . He's got prophecy behind him / and generations of Greek statuary." Yet, his perceptive eye marks out the sculpture's right hand, which is "blown all out of proportion," and he makes the metaphoric leap for us, giving it an ironic twist: "Heros beware, / lest you become heretical."

The third section, based on Donatello's rendition, works more like a film score, highlighting contrasts and dramatizing with poses and pop dialogue: "*So you send out this girl?* / The giant bellows in reply. / *Come to papa, Sweetie.*" In the middle of the poem, Minczeski compares the Bush administration to Goliath, once again using the myth to highlight how things remain the same because the stories repeat themselves: "You know the rest," he writes; "the lord sends rain to settle the dust; dogs wander through, / gnawing enemy corpses."

The final section of the poem uses Caravaggio's painting to show in Gothic detail a close-up of the severed head held in David's hand:

> Still bleeding out, it has not yet
> gone gray, this grotesque of Caravaggio's
> own head. Here, in the mirror that will not
> compromise, is your pride.

Art—the sculpture, the painting, the poem—is both mirror and self; and the self, divided, is both David and Goliath, both pride and humility, both strength and weakness. Both the oppressor and the oppressed, the killer and the killed. The self is made from the forgotten stories of those we will never know, of fragments and heaped memory.

In the end, we must embrace the paradox that is the broken body of the god. "What more did you expect?" Minczweski asks in the poem "Two White Bowls." In another poem, he seems to answer: "There is only this single, flexible moment: . . . olive trees on the hill, the same background / of a thousand paintings." Against this background, he has sketched out the lines which hint at a life—Serafin's life, and the reflection that is the poet's own life—the "few pigs, some rutabagas, and winter wheat," the descendants who are "heirs to [his] legacy of dirt," the wars and atrocities that play themselves out over and over, and the myths which both create and reflect our struggle against our inevitable return to dust.

SHARP STARS
by Sharon Bryan. BOA Editions, 2009. 104 pages. 6 x 9". $16.00. Paperback. ISBN-13: 978-1934414286.

"whoever [they] were."

The book ends on his great-grandfather's name, Serafin, as if a name could hold a fragment of that one life, even after it is gone. We see an insistence on speaking the names of the dead throughout the book: Romuald Minczeski who was given "a way out" by the Soviets "with a bullet to his head"; the names labeled in block letters on their belongings by the Jewish prisoners before they entered the showers at Auschwitz—of which Minczeski writes in a tone of deep sadness: "the tour keeps moving / I cannot copy more"; Leonarda, his great-grandfather's daughter who was so short she escaped the Gestapo's sweep for "defectives" by hiding among the very young, and who "taught children / to draw their [own] names." This relative became a familial myth, a woman who held "the hands of young widows / and "tracked / the decaying orbits of their dead."

Names also come into play with the ekphrastic poems woven throughout the book—the names of those gods and people who have lasted so much longer than the briefly lit candle of each individual life. Minczeski seems to be drawn to art that shows most clearly the breakage life encompasses: Leda and Zeus, Judith and Holofernes, Magdelene as a beggar woman, Theseus' abandonment of Ariadne, Michelangelo's Prisoners, the Madonna at the birth, and later, the Madonna at the death. In his poem,"The Last Pietà," he writes of Michelangelo's final work:

> Eighty years old, with little patience for fools
> or himself, he smashed the virgin's arm
> and the left leg of Jesus. Gone were the days
> he could wrestle a David out of flawed marble;

In these lines, we see how Minczeski's interest in art holds real life more dear than the myth; he shows the sculptor reflected in his work; shows how the darkness of age (or of an age) steals over even the greatest artist so that the artist himself creates the breakage, and then "the body of the god, / for the remaining eternity of stone, stays broken." Yet, Minczeski, with his perception of humanity's losses, also shows how Michelangelo's final honesty is what creates truth in his rendition of the receiving "Virgin—"her face gouged and unpolished, broad-cheeked / as a Polish peasant—she could be anyone's mother."

Minczeski's desire to bring things down to the level of the very real, flawed world (like the "flawed marble")—to where the Madonna is anyone's mother—is reflected in his language choices. His work displays a strange mix of real-world plain-speak contrasted with dramatic imagery—much like Caravaggio's style, if painting translated to writing, in that Caravaggio rejected idealization for contemporary realism. We see this clearly in his ekphrastic poem "The Davids," which takes on David as created by four artists: Bernini, Michelangelo, Donatello, and Caravaggio. This particular poem is compelling because the book looks so closely at loss and at "those broken / on the wheels of power." Thus, David as a mythic figure creates the necessary balance (and response?) to such suffering: he represents the idea that the weak, the oppressed, the hungry could overcome incredible odds and "put out buds for the future."

That said, what does such a figure look like? What does it take to have such courage of belief? What does it take to piece "the shattered fragments / of to materials at hand, including a peripatetic life in Virginia, Pittsburgh, Mexico City, the Philippines, Texas, and Nebraska; the bridge between languages (from Spanish and English and Tagalog); and the recognition that we are raised as much by culture (including art, television, movies, and more) as by family and community, Kristin Naca's *Bird Eating Bird* is about the ability to find the self in the varying manifestations of stories, whether the telling is under our control or not, and as such is a tribute to the enduring nature of the human character.

A LETTER TO SERAFIN
by John Minczeski. University of Akron Press, 2009. 72 pages. 6 x 9". $14.95. Paperback. ISBN-13: 978-1931968683

REVIEWED BY ARRA LYNN ROSS

Composed of five sections, John Minczeski's fourth collection of poems "plumb[s] the black soil" of his own family's Polish history to compile, if not a "harvest," a "heap"—something, at least, to bring for the "offering." Here, we find none of the "usual trickery" words can create, only a "shimmer" that makes one "wince," "hold up a hand to ward it off," and then, because one cannot stop the light from penetrating, one finds, the "world has changed."

Minczeski's heap is made from dug-up potatoes, old photographs, an October primrose, ekphrastic pieces about myths, from relics "we can't help but hoard," and fragments of his great-grandfather Serafin's last handwriting. Serafin's words reveal the heartbreaking reality of what it means to be human: "*it is not like being strong / this is our kind / not very tough.*" Despite this humble admittance, Minczeski's work refuses to shy away from the atrocities that riddle humanity's history— and the stories that back them up. In "Abraham," inspired by Caravaggio's *The Sacrifice of Isaac*, Minczeski writes in Abraham's voice, "For once, I'd like to ask why this business / of killing a son is so delectable. . . . For once, / I'd like to know what would happen if I declined."

Minczeski's delve into the past seems to be driven, in part, by a desire for resurrection—not salvation per se—nothing so "desperate" as "demanding eternity"; instead, he is looking for "part of [himself]" in the "acres of ruins" that remain after the "unmentionable harvest." As he asks at the end of his chilling sectional poem about his visit to the concentration camps:

> Did the circling angel of hope
> leave anything besides dust

His work, as a whole, takes up the answer to this question, offering, for a short span of time, the realization that one could be "thankful / words didn't disappear / into the cloistered future / the white noise of terra incognita." In spite of our being "bound to the chair of forgetting" like Pirithous, words— like the letter from Minczeski's great-grandfather Serafin—cross the divide of death and birth. Although "nothing remains the same . . . yet, everything remains the same" for there is "only one life," and this life is descended from those who came before, who fed the animals, and "gathered beets," and "set out sausage and relish,"

> they appear as brief, bluish
> swaths of paint, in a mirror
> that hangs in the background
> on a dark rear wall.

Art makes the world whole through beauty, even as it observes distinctions and corruption:

> All of us onlookers
> in the museum's corridor,
> standing beside the King and Queen,
> a troupe of royal attendees
> blued into existence by Velazquez, . . .
> giving the royals' yards of skin
> a taintedness—the illusion that,
> with every breath, they ingest
> the same bleak air we do,
> the room tinged with flecks
> of green and purple debris.

Naca follows this poem with "Becoming," a humorous comparison of entering a beauty contest with writing poems, as both are about image making.

The flipside of this unity is fragmentation—the dualism embedded in the reverberation between representation and reality, between story and life. Media culture's units of storytelling are beginnings, middles, and ends, which inflict false expectations on our own processing of experience. Hitchcock, Elvis, and J.R. Ewing haunt some poems like shadow selves from the collective unconscious, or boogie men from under the bed. The fourth wall dissolves in "While Watching *Dallas*, My Filipina Auntie Grooms Me for Work at the Massage Parlor" as the self stutters between how we see ourselves and how others see us, between what is, what was, and what could have been. "Rear Window," which picks up the thread of "Falling," is both persona and autobiography at the same time. Presented in Spanish and English, "Driving, I-80 Nebraska" telescopes the history of the settling of the Great Plains into the timeframe of a disconnected conversation:

> I rolled down the window and the breezes
>
> needled the wooly ends of used-up breath
>
> that had unspooled into the truck cabin.
>
> No hurry to tell the story as she drove.

The forms of story are many: myths, fables, history, and memory. They contain within them notions of character, setting, and plot, in a symbiotic and embryonic whole. Although we intellectually conceive of time as eternal, our firsthand experience of it is edited into discrete sections by the physical facts of our bodies and minds, that they grow, mature, and age. Using but not limited reimagined by successive generations, Naca's "Ode to Glass" loosely echoes his title "Having a Coke with You." Like another literary ancestor, Elizabeth Bishop, Naca finds her footing in a peripatetic life via focused attention on details. This poem is a sense memory, from a child's perspective, of drinking Pepsi. Through the reverent language of description the poem achieves its reward at the end, pinning the words down to a specific, locating event:

> Each time you drink—
> the bubbles rising up
> through the sweet,
> brown liquid, stirring
> your nose, then lips—
> how easily details
> of time slip away
> and you're seven-years-old
> again drinking Pepsi
> at the *sari-sari* store
> next to Uncle Ulpe's
> house in Manila. And
> you guzzle it down.

The functional violence of the men in "Baptism," who slaughter a pig in front of a girl, is echoed in the barbarism between genders and generations in "What I Don't Tell My Children About the Philipines." It also foreshadows Naca's fearless exploration of sexual language in "Tres Mujeres," the playful eroticism of "Glove," and finds mournful reverberation in the penultimate poem, "Catching Cardinals." Together, these poems of physicality honor the fragility of our corporeal vessels and their ability to survive the brutality of progression and dislocation that we experience as we mature and age.

Despite the world's sharp edges, such as the pig's "throat ridged and perfect / as a staircase" in "Baptism," these poems remain committed to beauty. Sensual, appreciative details float throughout, often in vivid descriptions of the sky, as in "before sunlight bathes the city in pink spells" of "Gavilán o Paloma" or the "Stars / so gravity cooked" of "Tres Mujeres," or the "vowels like a window to the throat" of "Uses for Spanish in Pittsburgh." In Naca's ekphrastic poem "Las Meninas / The Maids of Honor," Velazquez's portrait of a beautiful princess invites the viewer into art, and the art into the viewer: "I gaze and the Princess / gazes back through me." The borders of imagination and reality dissolve through creative achievement:

> The Infanta shows
> no regard for Velazquez
> who also gazes from inside
> the painting, onto the world
> that lay beyond the borders
> of the painting's framework.
> Somehow, Velazquez has
> captured that world, too.
> The King and Queen of Spain
> pose, there. Mere reflections,

Bird Eating Bird
by Kristin Naca. Harper Perennial, 2010. 112 pages. $13.99. Paperback. ISBN-13: 978-0061782343.

Reviewed by James Cihlar

Selected by Yusef Komunyaka for the National Poetry Series, Kristin Naca's debut poetry book, *Bird Eating Bird*, is a trans- and intercontinental travelogue of refracted identity and story. Composed of pristine vignettes set within the buzz of language gaps, gender divides, and media culture, this collection mythologizes the process of maturation. From a child's rapt and repulsed observation of men slaughtering a pig for a roast, to an adult's recollection of the delicate physicality of sex, these poems use persona, ode, portrait, and elliptical narrative to gain purchase on shifting ground. A compendium of approaches and experiments, including pantoum, syllabics, prose poems, as well as poems set in both Spanish and English, *Bird Eating Bird* achieves balance through calls and responses within the collection. Sifting languages outside of their origins, histories outside of their locales, Naca inscribes notes toward a manual on how to be manifold.

The book opens with "Speaking English Is Like," a catalog of similes whose lines float independently on the page. The poem embraces both the peremptory nature of the lexicon—"The staple that misfires and jams the hammer"—along with the seductive—"The tender, black wick at the top of a candle's waxy lip"—ultimately merging abortive and fecund directions in one line with "Endings that are dirty tricks and also feathers." The apparent randomness of order and repetition of syntax in this poem suggests the sense of striving and a drive for continuance that exists within the organism of language itself as well as in our varyingly successful attempts to use it. Naca praises this instinct in a later poem, "Seguir: To Follow, Keep On, Continue." And she places its complement, "Speaking Spanish Is Like," near but not exactly at the end of the book.

Disparate emotions occur simultaneously in the world of *Bird Eating Bird*. Affection and sorrow mark the approach of death in "Todavía No." Named after a song, "Gavilán o Paloma" ("Hawk or Dove") shows the two faces of love. "Uses for Spanish in Pittsburgh" both questions and asserts the language's valid place in an indifferent setting. When Naca's abstracted kaleidoscope settles on childhood reminiscences, a tenuously pleasant equilibrium enters the book, even with a commentary on class indicators embedded in a father's portrait:

> What use to remember in any language
> my father was a Puerto Rican shoe salesman.
> From his mouth dangled a ropy, ashy cigarette.
> He spoke good English and knew when to smile. . . .
> Still, I remember, he spoke a hushed Spanish
> to customers who struggled in English, the ones
> he pitied for having no language to live on.

The poem attempts to redress false assumptions by incorporating the use of Spanish.

If some of the other poems (such as "In Mexico City") in *Bird Eating Bird* perhaps more clearly trace their lineage to Frank O'Hara, as filtered and

Ralph Angel
Erasure

for Natsume Soseki

I don't want you to know about any of this. I probably changed. I was invariably
    disgusted with myself.

Then she began to talk deleriously. She lost her power of speech. When I got home
    she laughed.

I who had not remembered. What one says and what one thinks are entirely
    different things. Everytime I go outside

this is the price I paid.

It's blood that moves the body. Words aren't meant to stir the air only. They see
    somewhere in my heart

so long as my wife's
alive.

speak mostly to pigeons

and styrophoam

cups.

Get out.

Get out of my cab

he said. Wake up.

It's different.

RALPH ANGEL
Three Minutes and Sixty Years

A mere

shrug of atmosphere—

and then the fog

coughing up some buildings, and then

the smell of rain just inside

the door—

puts a naked eye

to things, and makes them

beautiful.

Losing

your phone is like

losing your mind. It's like

a fountain—

the door's wide open—

the words

tall buildings make

Friday

And I am losing language.
Taken with the strange
geography of the body. Agog. The lay
of the land so prescient and movable,
so pliant and usable.
(Something about the body and how you walk
around in it. How all the elements called *you*
are transported from sink to bed, car to pavement.)
How did I become my own
beast of burden? Carbon based, fuel hungry
– Automatic Response System?
Rapt, practically spellbound
by the all the gestures of modern life
dictated by circumstance; place hand here, wrap fingers
around shaft of spoon, rotate in a circular motion.
A congress of one, I am both audience and actor,
reader and writer. Egging myself on – I laugh
at all the right moments, shake my head in disbelief
at the predictable dialog and tired scenarios.
Look – a hand, an eye, the profile of a face.
Given the inability to see
inward, I hover above
my own topography. Barely attaining
an aerial view. Bee to my buzz, prop-
plane to landing strip, satellite to planet.
And all the while this is what the sign on my back said;
Applause now. House lights down. Exit stage left.

TINA SCHUMANN
Winner of the 2009 American Poet Prize

CALCULATIONS

> *No matter what you start out with*
> *you always end up with so much less.*
> —The Hours

Me –
the abridged, the novel that never was,
subtracted, abbreviated, some subtitle of self.
     So soon to be
the slightest signal of a woman, draped in my tattered flag,
holding a box of zeros
     and a mouthful of air.
When the end comes it won't matter.
     In between
I will have thought myself large, whole, my travels far,
experiences grand, many stories to tell and so on....
But what emancipation –
     to *be* diminished, reduced
to the absolute; a room deprived
of its contents, melting ice
at the bottom of someone's glass,
the tipped bottle and its residual remains.
     What delicious deliverance, –
what radiant resignation
to be
so much less
than I
could have ever hoped for.

were another thing   what
they said
          was true
                    the clouds of sky   said look
                                        past cloud and you're left
                                                                    with sky   look
                                                                    past sky and
                                                                    there's still
sky   birds fly
            left which means anger
            right which means gone   the closest
                                        I came to her
                                        was smoke   to breathe

                                        her again in who once smelled

                                                                  of milkflesh
                                                                  and wool

as long as the sky
is a color   I'll say
            blue she'll say
                        silver or green   and silver
                                          means a true
                                          love coming   or

                                          hail   and green
                                          in July a firstborn born

without fists   the birds
                        say danger   the birds
                                    say blame   bones
                                                of their flesh undressed
                                    men love
                                          fire

EMMA BOLDEN
THE WITCH'S DAUGHTER STILL LIVES

There were eyes   and eyes
and would she
bewitch like her witch

of a mother   would she
be a like one
to die   standing

that morning
with my new mother
I said the fire
was an angel   I said
it was the story of burning

straw into gold and the sparks
were fairies   I said someone

was making gold   she would not

take my hand   men love
fire and the bone it sings   men love
the heat sweet
it sings   after the fire
there are pieces
that cannot burn   there

are no
more eyes   there are pieces
of skull that once cradled
eyes   there is the stench

of hair in candle flame   she
in mass once
backed into a candle   and

as her hair cackled

they called her a curse

the bird wings

Unmarked Grave

> *All I want is a single hand,*
> *A wounded hand if that is possible.*
> —Federico Garcia Lorca

Beautiful man, with your brows of broken ashes
and eyes migrating the winter,

a hollow in your hand
where the moon fell through.

I could have kissed your mouth,
passed an olive with my tongue,
the aftertaste of canaries on our breath.

But the shriek of the little hour
is spent; there is no road back.

The day it happened
there were no good boys
or dovecots filled with virgins,

just a sun imploding
like a sack of rotten oranges,

the scent of basil
from the grove near your home
and the piano that still waits for you.

No one remembers
the coward who shot you,
but the sheets,

the white sheets you sail on,
coming home.

Lois P. Jones
The Swan's Flight

After the fire I found you still,
glowing amongst the ash. Here
at the bottom of the valley where mist

comes to cover bodies like sleeping gas.
Amber faces aflame with themselves
not yet fully burned, like a dream

you awaken in the middle of.
So many children curled and kept
from too much emptiness,

the calendars of the mind unturned
in a moment, the orange tree in flower,
a wind that sweeps down

over singed fields leaving its scar
in the grasses. There you were
at the centre of it all as I circled down –

my feathers full of flights,
of the unfinished journeys caught
on the cliffs – the only place I could land.

Clifton Gorge

There lives the dearest freshness deep down things… Gerard Manley Hopkins

Balsam floods the woods,
    swathing our senses
like moss swaddles roots and earth.
    Ferns flutter in the shadow
of the wind moving through,
    while we descend into the sanctuary
of the gorge like the sun lowers
    its long beams through the green
lattice of leaves above. We hope
    to hit bottom as the thrush

throws its deep voice across the crevasse.
    Where a woodpecker knocks on a door
of oak. And a lip of limestone loosens,
    tumbles down, greets us at the stream.
Which even now rips through rock,
    then pools its energy along the banks.
Where minnows animate
    the ruin, stirring the cup
brimming with revival, their small bodies
    flashes of hallelujah.

Keith Montesano
Variation on a Landscape

After Stephen Roach's Ajar

It begins with feigned invitation: preventing drunk driving,
        choking her because she has a knife, about to slit her wrists

                or yours. Always the excuse of opening: disorientation

and busted locks, black rooms and broken windows, as if
        we can go anywhere without warning, raid unfinished duplexes

                to plunge into veins, climb house frames in blackened ash

to find clues how they died. Or an excuse to enter
        the neighbor's backdoor, where she was *always naked, posing*

                like some goddess. Headlines composed of longing, testimonies

and court breakdowns, maps of entry and escape routes.
        Always some house on a tree-lined street. Always some neighbor.

                The bail and house arrest. Always repeating less than one year later.

Pyramid

We climb to rooftops
and spit our seeds on those below.

We see nothing above and think
Of course,
this is why heaven is highest!

Our buildings fly into stilled airplanes,
fish leap from cloud to cloud.

On the bottom of the world
our cities drip like icicles,

we lie on our backs
pretending the sky is down,
and try to fall.

Eleanor Swanson
Paradise

Hundreds of small green parrots
are hidden in the green schefflera
Paradise is full of trees—
ferny Poinciana, with deep
orange blooms, tissue purple
flowers of crepe myrtle,
gumbo limbos and date palms.

    Noon. Men tanned leather-skinned
work half-unseen in the feathery shade
of palms dividing their dumpster bounty.
Paradise. Is where you go to die
among the stone crabs and tuxedos.
"Dead artists don't eat," screams graffiti
trailing the walls of abandoned buildings.

    Then night. Neon—orange, purple,
pink, red, yellow—like the colors
of the flowers in paradise.
Flashing—blue, aqua, green—
like the water lapping
the beaches of paradise.
Sky the color of velvet
paintings, rivulets of silver
moonlight glazing the water.
Rumba rhythms, salsa, rock
blasting from beachfront bars.
Paradise is where you go
to party and forget.

    Midnight. Crossing a street
in Paradise one guy says
to another, "Last night
I was out of my body, just looking
down at it from somewhere.
I was out of my body, man,
and I didn't like it."

POST GRADS

Like *rōnin* minus the fighting prowess
and sense of honor, they wander
along highways and neglected railroads,
from town to town in search
of health care and a 2/2 teaching load.

Often we spot them in gazebos,
near wild geese or some manmade lake,
in Irish pubs that act like pockets
of hippy dissent in otherwise
all-white, right-wing college towns.

Know them by their red flannels,
their careful bangs and uncrossed legs,
their knowledge of Belgian beer.
Theirs are the cars in the parking lot
most desperately in need of brake pads.

When pressures burst, they retire
to bookstores and coffee shops, egos
propped over steamed milk,
hoping the next thing they see won't be
a former student's name in print.

But always they are drawn back
to classrooms the size of their apartments,
lectures on the Deep Imagists,
the pitfalls of verb tense and how to
salvage these endings, these heroic failures.

Michael Meyerhofer
WESTBOUND ELEGY

Buying canned coffee from a gas station
in the blur between night and day,
I decide I have not in ten years changed
despite all those costly lectures,
all these rhymes of fey aristocrats.
And the good sense of horses drawing close
from the chill of each fenced in field.
As for me, I must go on driving
beside a yellow line to somebody's funeral,
alone but for my gloves and credit card.
This is what passes here for fate:
the heart rests like a tire track
until men made out of paper undress us
and shovel us in fire, and we jump
straight up a stone neck towards the stars.

by memory I've spun my hair into shrouds
for masts of tibia, transfigured strands
into hawsers

holding an anchor, and halyards to hoist fragments of skull
polished to thinnest sails. Early evening
I finished my ship

with the last bone of a sheep's tail whittled
to a cabin pillar. On it I carved
a woman I glimpsed long

before this prison. Her hair whipped and curled like dark
myrtle on her neck, and splotches
of bright flowers

winked through as she turned from a field
to her carriage and now turns
to miniature

captain's quarters I breath into—a carriage
slowly suffused with the ghost
molting my chest.

David Thacker
French Prisoner of War Bone Ship, 1807

> *-Soldiers...you will again be restored to your firesides and homes; and your fellow citizens, pointing you out, shall say, "There goes one who belonged to the army...."*
> —Napoleon

Tonight, while the others sleep, I breathe into bones
softened by seawater that drizzles and pools
in the muck

of my cell, kiss a scrimshaw portrait I've etched—
cheekbones, smirk—, press again the cabin
of this model

to my lips, exhale a rattle. As a boy I raised
pigeons in a vaulted coop.
One bird squabbled

into flight, circled away, gray plumage shed
in my clutch. My cellmate wheezes
in sleep; he must

sprint behind dogs over sloping country
that hasn't deserted us. We scuttle,
knees in our hands,

lolling in an unknown port. A hulk seems
a hound of some mythic realm
and we, umbilicaled,

fetal young, gestate to aberrations: shoulders
slendered, arms folded to our sides,
faces thrust

forward—we are gulls, hens, or flightless doves
draped in rags. While my body
turns avian,

over the king-size and sprawls the long ceiling,

rakes the curtains, cockles the wallpaper, reframes
the photographs. Thorns burst open drawers and leaves enclose
my closet. And I, prince
of my black habitat, pluck

breakfast every midnight. I sew
my own blackberry clothes
with thimble fruits and needle thorns and smear
purple on my face and chest. I hang

my clothes on a torqued vine
to dry in July wind.
Someday soon, vested in canes, answering
no one, I'll be crowned the blackberry king.

David Thacker
Autonomy

    The canes rose over a ruck of green
        and gray guardrail,
     loped down an embankment, scaled
        a spruce and yield sign.

      A mythic heap
       like some spiny jellyfish
   far taller than a man
crouched against the sheared mountain. Berries dangled—a million

      miniature black-light lanterns. In a rush, I plucked,
was pricked and snagged,
         and I plucked—a fair economy of fruit, Levis,
skin, and blood. Now I rest and stretch with brimming

      tubs under eaves
   buttressing a low yew. The sky sifts through
the mesh of canes, thorns,
      and serrated leaves—the dark

screen of a dark door. An uncle told me once he saw a house possessed
        by bramble. I reach up,
   twist a thumb-sized knob, drop it
      in my mouth, and imagine a modest plant begin

   at the base of the chimney brick. It shoots,
    suckers, thickens, and climbs
the cedar shake. Some nightmare ivy gone up
      the house like lattice, roots swollen and hard,

    thick as doubled fists or femurs,
wooden tendons overlapping, a giant's gnarly wrist burst
  through deep loam. Fingers breach the home
     through an open bedroom window. I live

    in that house among the earth's barbed wire. This room—
my room. I wake early morning in a bed
        four-posted by bramble that bows

Clever not Beautiful

"If your goal is pure survival/ well then be clever, not beautiful..." H. Workman

My Cocteau mask is in the cellar where
Bachelard hides his desire to return to the womb.

I am writing transcripts for soldiers, technical manuals
For the dead programmers who refuse to leave the worms.

There is a special place for the wisdom – a god unto itself –
Spoils of foreign wars and new French bodies – the interest

In neo-postmodernism. I have left my shell for a topic.
I have found a man who designs babies for leftwing CEOs.

They will save the world with invaluable, cutting-edge research
As their posse shoot it up on Arctic melting ice, tag wings in Amazonian depths

Then get smashed on bootlegged brew in the exotic dance.
What the brilliance of our better selves can bring –

Can cure us of our fractal woes. What we know we eat like bodies
Of our own design and still believe in God.

MIKE WHITE
What Must Be

entire Ohio
emerges beyond the last
wisp of cloud, a feudal patchwork
of oblong kingdoms, variegated as a TV dinner.

In all Ohio I can see
one bleb of shine, a lone
car inching toward the horizon
and the afternoon sun going down.

And I can see a driver at the wheel, squinting into
a brown cadence of telephone poles and sagging lines
hooking the distance in between, tapping fingers in time
to whatever song is playing on the radio. A song I know, too.

Parking Lot, Pre-Dawn

The only light this hour
a sheen of crisp ice refracting
from last week's snow piles; someone

stepping onto crushed gravel, hips
barely brushing the grills of cars
as she drifts with a slow wobble

from one to the next, her gloved hand
leaving a three-pronged trail—thumb and pinky
float above the icy metal.

Watching, forehead to glass, you might imagine
you hear the frisson of fabric and frost.
You might in fact be lost

in the almost palpable almost-sound,
a vibration making its way to you until
the air is broken

by the helix of an alarm.
She stops. Then
as all of the proximal dogs weigh in

and the weak winter sun begins its ascent,
she sheds a pale scarf like a loose feather
before stepping toward the door—

open, as it must have already been—
and trailing the wings of her red coat,
plunges into the brief brightening there.

Alicia Vandevorst
Tepoztlan

The stair, underneath its exterior,
is a conveyor made of altars.
Each stone is a table that is bare
and your breath must be offered
as deeply as the steep incline
outside. The breath must reach far
inside to where it subsides at the bottom.
That is the stone as it accepts the gift—
the emptiness between this and this,
where love permits a transference of rhythms.

There is

a constant endearment between feet and stone
as if the weight of a body is a fragrant orange
your heart sets down
on each stone
and this sameness of reverence
makes the stair one step,
one act with only tiny increments,
nothing to accumulate and stress the breath.
Each step is a perfect rest.

At the End of the Day

They said,
& it was cliché—
nothing rose from the horizon
      no moon, no revelation.
& they meant
      whether we were safe or not,
           the train would come on schedule,
                bats would dive for ultrasonic prey.
The phrase was vapid
      & they used it up.
At the end of the day
      became the key to the kingdom.
          & all that had gone before drowned there,
         all that followed
              died its own meaningless death—
the yard mouse's eye sockets crawling
    with stars and planets.

Phoebe Reeves
The Folly of Mercutio in a Pacifist Town

The emperor moth battles the emperor
penguin, 2 to 1 knockout, no
terms, no surrender. Darwin
officiates—aren't we all charming
in the ballroom where everyone
under twenty texts
without looking at their hands,
some literal synecdoche. Fluid
cyborg semiotics lost on poor
emperor at his victory
banquet where we squander
the horizon as if it were
devalued currency, bringing it in
wheelbarrows, trading it for shot glasses
that say "I ♥ the Emperor" and
drinking cheap gin in daring rounds.
Meanwhile we are navigating ever
more backwards towards a
musky gray that barks at us and
pees ominously on the banquet
tables. What can be done? The
emperor moth longs for icebergs;
the lolling beaten penguin's
heart seizes up with thoughts of
August's sizzling porch lights.

We follow Rt 80 like a bead of water on a thread,
drawn west through the impregnable Alleghenies,
median swollen with color—black-eyed Susans,
Queen Anne's Lace, chicory annihilating the blank
canvas of grass with their hue and texture.

Oblique slant of wind as truckers pass.
In the car, my fingers dream of orchids
and sandalwood. The median flowers
open and shut their eyes in my chest over
and over.

Phoebe Reeves

from The Paradox of Names

Twelve: Zenaida macroura

Everything bleeds earthward, to impart
ironic tang to our salads, our loaves.
This twist is better than salt, the interregnum
between death and consumption.

Dark shirts trailing sandalwood.
Shadowed corners hold gardenias in cut glass
and artesian water. The annihilation of the market place.

In the morning, the trees have grown sockets
on their lower limbs, where incandescent
bulbs now screw in tightly and incandesce.
The birds lay below them in tanning bed posture.
The squirrels try to unscrew them and there after
the afternoon smells slightly of scorched squirrel.

We are as ruthless as the world around us.

It's easy to annihilate the 4x4 patch of blooms,
cucumber flowers already wilting & unfruited,
the tacky bold sunflowers half bent in reverence, in
anguish. One pass of the rototiller and this
all turns under into the past.

Fields redolent with meadowsweet, a hillside's
white fringed sartorial attitude. June
soaks in its longest suns, turning slowly on itself.

2.

*Gentle Abel, do not stir,
we will lend a coat of fur...*

That's how when fever addled
your infant brain I'd sing to you.

Now sleep is strung with maggots
that fiddle through the flintholes.

O Eden! Rocks become cradle!
Pour his blood from your soil,

fruit the tree I planted over him
and water it since I can't return...

I rule a metropolis. The son after
whom I named the city follows me

with your eyes as if he knows
the words to my unsung lullabies.

Cursed from the ground, if not
for this permanent stain

by now my flesh would pillow
your bones as chaff to grain.

NOD

1.

The first brothers in history—
how was I to know to give

a damn? Whenever we spoke
with god, the boy cajoled him,

left me stuck with my stammer.
If only I hadn't looked so much

like father. And mother—
a twice-shy snakecharmer playing

favorites from day one. Anyway,
compared to sowing crops

by hand what is it to pen
a drowsy herd of sheep or two?

You'd think he made his bed
in the barn the way he wore

lanolin like a perfume, yet
before his burnt offerings—

ribs thrice weekly, no less—
I should wash? One day, he kept

sharpening a particular flint until
I thought the blade would snap…

"For sacrifice," he said, the last
either of us spoke to the other.

Fugitive

Your wife's sweet distances:
       Where are they?

      Last night you slept next to her,
and through a sliver of open curtain,
you watched the sensual strip
          tease of the moon.

At that hour, you wanted to be water
drinking itself, not water

      afraid of freezing. In that quiet
both of you were an abandoned project
a greater mind couldn't finish.

      You're driving now through another
Texas town.
          Dust holding things
in place like a ribcage. The light
hard as granite.

Octavio Quintanilla
Suicidas

They came and found only the lint of my voice.
Then they were gone.
I want to talk about them,
these wretches who leave their feathers
all over the furniture, who,
in my absence, plaster the walls
with insomnia.

They leave their clumsy anger
at the foot of my bed, all over
the toilet seat. An earring
on the kitchen floor, evidence
they are human.

This time I find only the sewer
stench abandoned by someone in a hurry
to get elsewhere. Whoever they are,

they have taken
my pillow and have bent and twisted
a coat hanger into a cross.
They have taken my hope and the last
of my children, but have left no instructions
on how to get them back.

I want to talk about them.
I want the stammering of their hands to stop.
"Don't come back," I say, "Don't come back,
for I've forgiven the doorways
that let pass all that we love."

what we are
twin to gold
what we are
closer still
twins we are

Kevin Simmonds
THE SINGING

allow some
to fall away
let it fall
twin to dust
what we are
twin to water
what is meant
to fall away
let's consent
to fall away
what is meant
twin to dust
twin to gold
human lord
faraway
let it fall
closer still
what we are
what is meant
to fall away
everywhere
is closer still
everywhere
to fall away
let's consent
to what is meant
human lord
twin to gold
twin to dust
allow some
closer still
to fall away
allow some
to fall away
let them fall
let's consent
to what we are
human lord

Tobacco

We cannot get rid of the smell:
kitchen rising with bread

baked half an hour too long,
the weeds of field like crust

growing into the recess of oven.
All around us the sun shakes

leaves so bright they burn a green
flame over the skirts of land.

Out back, rows of crops
sweep themselves into tidy

borders of sky. When no one
is looking, they speak

through stalk rumblings of sound,
curling their stem of tongues

like fists through air.
Sleepwalking, they travel

at night through the strains
of drought, digging beneath dirt

and roots in search of some way
to keep breathing out—

the inhale, exhale
of the obtruding seasons.

Antelope

scouting the tiny creases of your mouth
for a space to write my name
I come undone by the arch of your back
the victory applause between your legs

your body is a broken silence
far across the morning   words
fall from the claws of hungry doves
and your heart spreads like antelope

while I'm hidden in the bushes
searching for a new forensics
lost beneath initials and thumbprints
the distractions passed off as love

caught on spare branches
air and space fought for

every evening

    *

substation warning lights
dip in the distance
vast all our carbon remains
breathing in time

with the carriage sway

track clicks our measure
light flickers in darkness
final actions boxed objects
dissolve in due course

outlines

>   hair
>   tooth
>   and
>   nail

but we
do not own this
we are not planters

we are transit
from one place to the next

aiming our greetings
and appointments

at satellites
and outposts

at the end of imagination

Alan Jude Moore
Dark Green Water

this dark green water
dulled by rain clouds
hung over rusted
barn buildings and outhouses

corrugated shelters
barely standing
by rested rolling stock
and motorway plumage

cable
        lines
                broken

pieces of tile and porcelain
scattered on the tarmac
in heaps behind the depot
will be washed away

into effluent and leaves
become ancient someday
buried in the groundswell
fingerprints erased

        through units of foliage
flow slightly towards the road
between cattle batches
and cellular masts

deep behind the fields
bells ring   hopefuls
hobble up and down
stone streets and the small
city walls

seeds to be sown

tired pools of nightmare
reflect the spectrum

Rachel McKibbens
Overheard at the Cannibal Cafe, Union Square NYC

"Misogynist: A man who hates women as much as women hate one another"
—Henry Louis Mencken

He stumbles into the diner
clutching a throat of roses.
She looks up from the menu
and smiles like a dead movie star.
Her eyes, a dark potion. His face,
a spoiled clock. He takes the seat across from her,
placing his top hat next to the salt shaker.
A silence snaps the air. As he waits for her to speak,
he measures his love in skin: her shiny square nose,
her missing arm & sloppy tits.
When she puts down the menu
a bloated rat scrambles across the floor
and dies at her feet. The waitress takes his order,
then nods to the woman: *How about you, honey?*
She bites her lip then shrugs. Her voice
is a tarnished guillotine:
Something female, I guess.

Rachel McKibbens
Selachimorpha

Billy, whose father sells firecrackers to kids
from an ice cream truck, makes you touch it in
the empty locker room. When you start to cry, he
grabs you by the hair and forces you to learn the salt
of another boy before you ever kiss a girl. You hide
in your room for eleven days until they find your sister
dead on Grove Street. The children come running
to your door. The police man lets you ride in the front seat.
Once you break through the crowd, you find a girl-shaped
puddle of salt water wearing a soggy green dress
and white Mary Janes filled with sea shells.
The bad news drops your mother to the pharmacy floor.
She cracks her head open, spilling teams of hermit crabs
that scuttle out the door. At the first funeral, your father
cries himself into a mound of wet sand. Nobody notices
you build a castle from him. The kids at school
tease you, leave a dead squid in your gym bag,
dump a pail of fish heads onto your desk.
When the vice principal finds you tied to
the fence at the end of the football field
with makeshift gills cut into your torso,
you tell him you didn't see the faces of those
who attacked you. When they burn your house down,
you stand in the front yard to watch with the neighbors.
As the sirens turn the corner, you make your way
to the house at the end of the street. You watch
Billy through his bedroom window. He is petting his dog
and watching television. You bite your lower lip until a tooth
breaks through. Then another. And another. A gutter of blood
collects in your mouth. A sharp pain shoots from your spine
and a fin pops out of your skin, smooth and dorsal.
Your flesh greys into a thick slick suit.
Your eyes become shining black marbles.
You smell Billy's thrashing heart from eight feet away.
When the caudal fin bursts from your tailbone,
you know what it is, without even looking.

Mill City

No human echo—
Just a hum that drips from the street

wires, a pulse that lets loose
from the glass of vacant storefronts.

My mind is filthy with old, dear secrets.
Another room sinks into its pine boards

and someone comes to assign value;
pull sewage out of the canal.

So much left over from so much
ordinary life.

I am seduced
by the red X on buildings

where no one bothers. Another ceiling
gives in and my gutters fill.

It is the unlit room,
the windowpane that keeps hold

of that flat ochre light.
It is absence.

And not even post and beam can escape
the flutter of that grey wing.

A crack opens another foundation—
Something in the flesh trying to beat its way out.

Just watch it go.

Lia Brooks
Here it comes, a feather

I prefer this to your leaf.
When I pull it through my hand
it flicks back into shape perfectly.
The grey-white plume resembles a pen
as it does flight and it is
a door that I am jealous of.

We bring the trees in, create a woodland
in our living-room. When the start
of our garden is undetermined
I resemble a crab, the very salmon of it,
shell corroded. All barnacle and salt
to the claw and out of place. I see him better

in the branches, rushing leaves to the ceiling.
He turns like bark mapping hazel,
spills hand-spans of rust and maroon,
covers our coffee table. I touch the open
wound where a leaf left him. He tells me
he prefers leaves falling— when a feather falls
it reminds him of a cat. As evening lifts an owl

through the shadows of the hall I claw
what I can, burrow in the sandy cool
of the kitchen lights like a thief
with a harvest of clams. I hear cormorants
call from the stone range, shore slowing
on windowpanes. When he sleeps with acorns

and waterfalls, coral and waves tumble
our floorboards, the gull's grey-white wing
leaving a feather to dip the bluest inkwell.

Winter

the stars tonight have unearthed their dead roots
and teeter on the pillars of the sky
as though about to fall–because, unbalanced

their fibers were undone and stitched together
by the flux of our attentive eyes
like the occasional polishing of shoes

while I, underneath these many pews, behold
the fecund seeds contained inside those white
and void cartesian points, impossible

to scale: to watch them slowly burn

Sandra Kohler
Summons

Surprise always, the day wakes us, the dream,
the night. The hard knock of rain against rattling
casements or the light's slow filtering beneath
shuttered blackness. The new lies on the old, with
the old, like the telling trail of river fog through
autumn's hard sharp air, speaking its gray name
along a whole horizon. What we reclaim is never
open as what we desire. You dream the house you
are looking at will not suit: it has low ceilings and
you will never give up your high rooms. This is
a fable you have decided to live in, inscribed in
your own hand. But the one written for you, in
a scrawl you can't decipher, an alphabet that seems
unfamiliar, is a darker story, richer. It can sustain
the lowest ceiling of all, a coffin, or open to a depth
you've not begun to imagine. Summons will come
soon enough, rough and brutish as the touch of
winter. What you will do when the phone rings,
the doorbell, you still don't know, though you
have rehearsed this scene before yesterday's vain
mirror and the damning glass of tomorrow.
The morning star has disappeared, sun is a faint
rumor. What won't marry maybe, when refuses
the petition of why. How will you know this place
when you come to it again? By the hard knock of
rain, the rough touch of winter, the glint of light
off wires that string one pole to another, a web
broken and incomplete as anyone's life.

Seascape

She was sure the air was drowning her. In the night, the seaweed crept in her window, choking her. She woke gasping for breath. Even miles away the air, reeking of tar and saline and decaying algaes, carried the feathers of dead gulls. And the way the seals watched her, curious, distant, as if she too were about the float out in the water, one more rotting thing in the sea. Even the otters began to bare their teeth at her while they played on the boat docks, and the crows became more numerous. She did not dare walk barefoot on the ocean shore, not any more, now that the warm sand had given way to slippery, jagged rocks, the way the wind stung her throat and skin. The sticky salt left a trail on her she could taste. She broke the backs of black and white bees, brushed off creeping sea beetles and green spiders. The kingfishers tutted at her to "leave, leave." She gathered things in her hands to hold onto. She stopped thinking of the sea as escape.

Rebecca Kinzie Bastian
The Heart is a Flock of Starlings

:dark rush against blue sky. Plain faced and speckled, each bird beats,
knows the singular sound of voice, feels wind hard against wings.

: a door, a window, a gate, the tunnel in, out–a flock of starlings opens and closes
like those doors, like a fist, like the valves of the thing it is.

: palpitating mass of one and one and one, plain as the road
you're driving on when you see them and stop, open mouthed at the sheer numbers.
That is your desire up there, you know it and gasp at the sad/plain/shining flight.

: tight but open, one but individual, plain but glossy backed
and beautiful. Listen to its chirping, disappointment's resonance, love and color lifting
as one great sweep. Loud noise for such small wings.

(Of a Dinner) Begin Violently

*

Colonies of bacon wrapped deep-come kingdom,

a table set for perpetuity. We have corn. We have

rolls—crisscrossed or (hot) Royce, outside or (cross'd) buns;

Turn off the television, the good china. *Eat.*

*

Icing frozen drips like carnival of lighthouses,

today is your birthday. *Over here, Over here,*

Flash (flash), Flash (flash), smile, *say cheese.*

And you say what kind? And everyone laughs.

So much of what we immerse, we dunk underwater first.

*

Words like *fresh, steamy, fogged*. The windows outline

ghosts. The car in the driveway. We have winter weight

(a slip of money, a prayer) all our limbs thick with aftermath,

with warning. Here are the potatoes. Here is the gravy.

The Shaded Areas Are Plots For Gardens and Graves

A cartographer sketches your ventricles

on the outside of your skin

(bloomblack and orange pistil)

*

Unfurl a flower caught on film

played backwards and forwards

(on repeat)

*

How petals burgeon, dissolve.

When you exhale your map, I love you less

(loam and sully, roots and wither)

In The Middle Of The Middle Of

(No one lives in

that house.) A foghorn in mist, pockets

full of mortar, cedar and rust. Inhale

weight in pounds of minnow's school,

a marrow full of five thousand siblings,

five thousand ways to disappoint.

A window's school of waves, hands

that learn to wave hello. An eventual diploma

of interrelated allergies, signal phrases.

(No one has lived there for years.

                      No one lives in

that house.)

Salty lips on the loose brick stairs,

a game of disintegrated ground-swallow,

every pastel earth tone imaginable.

Look out over the hill, down the road,

look at that view. O haunting of matte

and glossy, coiffed and crumbling.

A nightly prayer for the dying,

the already dead. (No one lives in

        that house anymore.

No one lives there.)

ARRA LYNN ROSS
    on *The Poet's Cookbook: Recipes from Tuscany*
        by Grace Cavelieri and Sabine Pascarelli **74**

CONTRIBUTORS. **76**

Aleah Sato
    CLEVER NOT BEAUTIFUL............................35
David Thacker
    AUTONOMY..36
    FRENCH PRISONER OF WAR BONE SHIP, 1807..........38
Michael Meyerhofer
    WESTBOUND ELEGY.................................40
    POSTGRADS.......................................41
Eleanor Swanson
    PARADISE..42
Matt Summers
    PYRAMID...43
Keith Montesano
    VARIATION ON A LANDSCAPE........................44
Julie L. Moore
    CLIFTON GORGE...................................45
Lois P. Jones
    THE SWAN'S FLIGHT...............................46
    UNMARKED GRAVE..................................47
Emma Bolden
    THE WITCH'S DAUGHTER STILL LIVES................48
Tina Schumann
    CALCULATIONS....................................50
    FRIDAY..51
Ralph Angel
    THREE MINUTES AND SIXTY YEARS...................52
    ERASURE...54

Reviews
JAMES CIHLAR
    on *Bird Eating Bird* by Kristin Naca..................55
ARRA LYNN ROSS
    on *A Letter to Serafin* by John Miczeski..............58
EIREANN LORSUNG
    on *Sharp Stars* by Saron Bryan........................61
DANIELLE SELLERS
    on *Temper* by Beth Bachmann..........................63
ARRA LYNN ROSS
    on *Carpathia* by Cecilia Woloch......................65
MERYL DEPASQUALE
    on *By Myself: An Autobiography*
    by D.A. Powell and David Trinidad..................67

JOHN DEMING
    on *Wait* by C.K. Williams............................69
DAVID DOODY
    on *Ghost on 3rd* by Jim Reese.........................72

The American Poetry Journal
Table of Contents

POETRY

Katie Jean Shinkle
    IN THE MIDDLE OF THE MIDDLE OF............... 7
    THE SHADED AREAS ARE PLOTS FOR GARDENS
        AND GRAVES........................ 8
    (OF A DINNER) BEGIN VIOLENTLY.................. 9

Rebecca Kinzie Bastian
    THE HEART IS A FLOCK OF STARLINGS........... 10

Jeannine Hall Gailey
    SEASCAPE......................... 11

Sandra Kohler
    SUMMONS........................ 12

William F. Holden
    WINTER........................ 13

Lia Brooks
    HERE IT COMES, A FEATHER................ 14

Kate Hanson Foster
    MILL CITY..................... 15

Rachel McKibbens
    SELACHIMORPHA..................... 16
    OVERHEARD ATH THE CANNIBAL CAFE, UNION
        SQUARE NYC....................... 17

Alan Jude Moore
    DARK GREEN WATER........................ 18
    ANTELOPE........................ 20

Kerri French
    TOBACCO 21

Kevin Simmonds
    THE SINGING...................... 22

Octavio Quintanilla
    SUICIDAS..................... 24
    FUGITIVE..................... 25

Christian Nagel
    NOD..................... 26

Phoebe Reeves
    FROM THE PARADOX OF NAMES............. 28
    THE THE FOLLY OF MERCUTIO IN A PACIFIST TOWN 30

Judith Skillman
    AT THE END OF THE DAY.................... 31

Alicia Vandevorst
    TTEPOZTLAN..................... 32

Rebecca Aronsen
    PARKING LOT, PRE-DAWN................ 33

Mike White
    WHAT MUST BE 34

Editor:
J.P. Dancing Bear

Reviews Editor:
James Cihlar

Advisory Board:
Jennifer Michael Hecht
Bob Hicok
Jane Hirshfield
C. J. Sage
Diane Thiel

Subscriptions:
Individuals: $20.00 per year
Institutions: $25.00 per year
(Please add $6.00 postage per year for subscriptions outside the United States.)

Web site: www.americanpoetryjournal.com

**The APJ reads magazine submissions online only.
Please see website for the latest guidelines.**

Address submissions, queries, orders, and all other correspondence to:

J.P. Dancing Bear, Editor
The American Poetry Journal
Post Office Box 2080
Aptos, California 95001-2080

The American Poetry Journal Copyright 2004 - 2011 All Rights Reserved
ISSN 1547-6650
ISBN 978-1-935716-07-5

Cover art: "Jewel Harp" courtesy of Timothy Martin
www.timothymartin.com

The American Poetry Journal is a production of Dream Horse Press LLC

The American Poetry Journal

APJ

Issue number Ten

www.ingramcontent.com/pod-product-compliance
Lightning Source LLC
Chambersburg PA
CBHW031632160426
43196CB00006B/383